So You Want to Publish a Book?

This is the half title page.

This is the title page.

So You Want to Publish a Book?

Anne Trubek

Belt Publishing

This is the copyright page.

Printed in the United States of America
First edition 2020
1 2 3 4 5 6 7 8 9

ISBN: 978-1-948742-66-5

This is the Belt colophon.

Belt Publishing
3143 W. 33rd Street #6
Cleveland, Ohio 44109
www.beltpublishing.com

Cover by David Wilson
Book design by Meredith Pangrace

CONTENTS

So You Want to Publish a Book?

Introduction

When I was in high school, I wrote bad poetry, as teenagers are wont to do. I wrote thinly veiled poems about boys I had crushes on, and pretentious poems about the passage of time. One overwrought lyric was about my disappointment upon looking at the author photo on the back of a poetry collection—I am pretty sure it was Wallace Stevens—and seeing the wizened face of the author. I remember my terribly clever last line: "Poets should never be old."

I tell you this because it tells you something important about me: by sixteen, I was already fascinated by, and opining on, the material elements of books and how they connect to our ideas about what writing is. We may have presuppositions about a book's author, but once we see an actual photo on a piece of paper that shows what the author looks like, we confront the contrast between our ideas about an author and the author's actual appearance.

Writing is both a thing and not a thing; material and immaterial. Letters and ideas. Imagination and paper. Knowledge and a commodity. This has always obsessed me during my zig-zaggy career from English professor to freelance writer to book writer to magazine founder to publisher. The beauty of writing has resided in its immateriality, its ability to transcend place and time, weight and mass. It is not the thingness that gives writing its power; it is its ability to escape any grasp. But for writing to be nothing, it must inevitably (and paradoxically) be embodied, made into a thing. A scrap of paper. A screen that contains pixels. Something inked, or pressed, or carved. Arbitrarily chosen marks that correspond to sounds. Stuck between boards or lit by browsers. And sometimes, something accompanied by a photo of an individual who, somewhere else, at some other time, created those marks.

These seemingly opposing dichotomies are the through line of my career. I started thinking about how we make writing into things in college, and I continued to do so while I was a PhD student in English. Then I became a college professor and wrote books—*A Skeptic's Guide to Writers' Houses* and *The History and Uncertain Future of Handwriting*—that took up different aspects of this obsession. Eventually, I left academia and started Belt, my own publishing company. Some people, looking at my CV, laugh about how various and unexpected it is: a few years ago, I was a tenured professor at Oberlin College; today, I run a small press focused on the Rust Belt. Along the way, I have edited a textbook on writing technologies, written books on writers' house museums and the history of handwriting, and edited collections of essays about Cleveland and the Rust Belt. Now a publisher, I oversee the making of books. So far, only two people have been able to figure out the connective thread running through my career on their own.

"You are obsessed by the materiality of books," they told me. I almost cried, both times, when these strangers revealed they had figured out the puzzle.

So if my path to becoming a publisher seems like a winding one, it has actually been relatively straight, in that the same central idea has always driven and fascinated me. I have never worked for another publishing company. But I have spent my life staring at author photos, studying the history of the book in the West, traveling around the country visiting museums dedicated to writers, and researching the different tools humans have used to make letters, words, sentences, and paragraphs over many centuries. The fact that I now spend most of my days editing, typesetting, talking to printers, assigning ISBNs, entering metadata, sending out press releases, and shipping paper to customers isn't all that surprising.

This is a section break.

———————

Being obsessed with a rather arcane concept like writing has made things difficult for me at points, both for chitchat and in interviews. When I have been lucky enough to have journalists interested in a book of mine, the first question I am often asked is, "How did you get interested in that?" I have found if I respond with, "Reading a lot of Roland Barthes in college," or, "I've always been fascinated by the materiality of writing," the questioner either assumes I am dodging or rejects the answer as not making good copy. They'll ask again for some personal story that sparked my obsession. Did I have bad handwriting in elementary school? Did my dad take me to Ernest Hemingway's house when I was a kid? Or maybe it all has to do with being a mother? "What's the real reason?" they implore, with their tone and their looks. I want to reply, "A LIFE OF THE MIND CAN BE A REAL REASON!" but that answer would only be critiqued, accurately, as snobbish. So instead, I invent some biographical answer and hope to move on.

Finding an answer to this question isn't any easier now that publishing books, rather than writing them, consumes most of my time. It is difficult to describe what I do now too. "I publish books" is a sentence that could refer to either writing or producing books. So instead I reply with, "I am a publisher." This answer pains me, though, because it sounds so passive. But when I say, "I am a publisher," no one is confused if I'm referring to writing books or to making the physical accoutrements to embody words. Nor, thankfully, does anyone ask me for the "real" reason why I am a publisher. It seems that you don't need a personal backstory in order to decide to finance the material creation and dissemination of the written word.

This confusion over the verb "publish" explains the title of this book, which I've written for writers as well as for prospective publishers (as well, of course—I hope!—for experienced authors, people in the publishing world, and anyone curious about the inner workings of a culture industry). The implied "you" in the title might be addressed to a range of people with similar questions: What does a publisher do? How does a writer secure a book contract? How do designers, editors, and publishers transform a Word document into paper that is bound by boards, stamped with a barcode, and sold to consumers?

Despite a lifetime of reading about books and their histories, I had a very fuzzy conception of my job as a publisher before I actually started doing it. Scholars, going all the way back to Plato, have spent far more time researching what it means to read or write than they have researching what publishers—who serve as the crucial conduit between those two activities—actually do. Going through the process of writing books that were published helped me understand the publishing process in its barest outlines, at least from the author's point of view. But it was only once I decided to sit on the other side of the desk—acquiring, editing, and printing instead of being acquired, edited, and printed—that I really started to understand the industry.

I am still learning what being a publisher is all about, as well as what being published means. I started by publishing a book that was meant to be a singular project, *Rust Belt Chic: The Cleveland Anthology*. Then, I was curious about the rise of self-publishing and excited that it was possible to turn a manuscript into a printed, bound commodity oneself. So I paired my interest in the city of Cleveland with my interest in teaching myself a bit about publishing. Then I decided to make that first book into a series of sorts, publishing anthologies about Detroit, Cincinnati, Youngstown, and other Rust Belt cities. A few years later, I looked up and realized I was running a press. Along the way, I had a printer refuse to run copies of a book because it contained a cartoon of a naked man (the owner of the printing company was a fundamentalist Christian, worried about his other clients); learned how to have books distributed by a wholesaler only to have that company go bankrupt, leaving me unpaid for books that people had bought; and had to drive all night with cartons of books in the trunk of my car when a book suddenly sold far more than we anticipated. I also got better at working with designers, promoting our titles, and working with independent booksellers. I developed a mission for the press and a set of principles for what we would publish or not, and found, lost, and found again people to work with who understand what Belt is about. They helped Belt slowly become a "real" business that now makes enough money so that tax time is confusing.

My experiences are not comprehensive; they're decidedly idiosyncratic. Publishing insiders will no doubt dispute some of what I write in this book, and in no way should this book be approached as a "manual" with anything beyond anecdotal authority. But what I can offer those who are interested in publishing, however that word is used, is a peek behind one small curtain, to show you how the company I founded and direct works, how I proposed books and had books proposed by others, and the promises and perils I see in the current publishing landscape. The "you" of the title will shift: some chapters, like Chapter Two, assume you're a writer who would like to publish nonfiction; others, like Chapter Three, on how much books cost to make, assume you're interested in becoming a publisher or learning how one part of the industry works. In other chapters, I may be talking more to those who work in or write about publishing and books. But all these "yous" can be encompassed in one larger person: someone who is curious and interested in the business of books.

The genesis for this "part handbook, part argument, part memoir," as the thumbnail review might call this book, was a newsletter, *Notes from a Small Press*, I started in October 2018. Each week I wrote about one aspect of publishing, aiming to help people understand my job and American publishing in general. I also wanted to vent frustrations, extol triumphs, and muse about the curious job I have made for myself. This book builds upon those newsletters, and its goals are the same. First, I want to reveal the inner workings of one independent publisher in order to aid transparency, which I believe is a huge factor in increasing access to publishing. I believe understanding book publishing from behind the scenes will enable more people to have a part in it, whether as an author, editor, publicist, designer, or publisher.

This book will not, however, help you write a book. (There are plenty of other great books out there that do that!) The publishing process, not the writing one, is my main focus. I discuss how books are designed and financed, promoted and printed. I discuss how nonfiction book contracts often come to be, but I spend little time on fiction, as that is outside the purview of most of my experience.

This book does provide insight into and makes an argument about American book publishing in the early twenty-first century, which is dominated by multinational conglomerates who produce books that are sold by a monopolistic retailer, Amazon. Independent presses and booksellers are interrupting what is becoming a scarily monopolistic pipeline. I want these interruptions to become louder and longer, and in the chapters to come, I explain how and why this might happen. So this book is also for anyone who values heterogeneity, complex and original thinking, and aiding those who are too often blocked by gatekeepers to walk through those doors.

CHAPTER ONE:

The Lay of the Publishing Landscape

A Note on Terminology

Terminology for types of presses can be very confusing, so for the purposes of this book, here's how I will be using some key terms:

A **traditional publisher** is a press that underwrites all costs to produce a book and offers authors advances and/or royalties. There are several types of traditional presses, distinguished by how large they are or what business model they use.

A **nontraditional publisher** typically asks clients to underwrite some of the costs, and can include vanity presses, hybrid presses (a hybrid between traditional and self-publishing), or self-publishing.

The **Big Five,** or "**conglomerate publishers**," are owned by multinational corporations. They publish the largest percentage of traditionally published books.

An **independent press** is not owned by an outside company or corporation. Often used interchangeably with **small press**, independent presses can be quite large: Norton and Scholastic are both independents, for example. An independent press might be either for-profit or a nonprofit. A trend in small presses concurrent with conglomeration is the rise of nonprofit publishers, such as Graywolf, Coffee House Press, and McSweeney's. Also included under this umbrella are university presses, which are nonprofits because they are owned and operated by universities. Many independent presses are for-profits, but are also focused on a mission (like most independent bookstores are); examples include Europa Editions, Verso, City Lights, Grove, New Directions, and Belt Publishing.

Self-publishers sometimes refer to themselves as independent publishers, which can create a wake of confusion. Self-publishers are not traditional publishers, however. The key distinction might most simply be boiled down to money: who pays the bills for editing, printing, and distribution costs? If it is the publisher, then the book is traditionally published, be it by a conglomerate or independent press, or a for-profit or nonprofit for tax purposes. If the author pays, then it is some variety of nontraditional or self-publishing.

Quick: name the publisher of that American classic, *Moby-Dick*. Stumped? Try Toni Morrison's *Beloved*. No? Okay—how about a recent bestseller, such as *Twilight, Gone Girl*, or Michelle Obama's *Becoming*? Still stumped? Maybe we should return to some classics: who published *The Catcher in the Rye, To Kill a Mockingbird, Light in August*?

Okay, any book at all. Can you name any publisher for any book at all?

Probably not. Publishers, strangely, are enigmas in the book world. Very few if any American presses have recognizable identities to laypeople, and most readers do not register the colophon (the publisher's brand) when they're considering which book to read or remembering a book they loved. There are exceptions: some publishing houses have more of a brand identity than others. FSG, or Farrar, Straus and Giroux, often connotes quality. Many associate beat poetry with City Lights, Norton with doorstop anthologies assigned in college, Penguin with classics, Verso with radicalism. But even this list is likely too "inside-publishing" for most people. Those associations also may not resonate with people whose jobs orbit around books, including librarians, booksellers, professors, reviewers, and authors themselves.

Why do publishers have such faint reputations? Other culture producers suffer similar problems—do you know who records and releases Taylor Swift's albums? Which gallery represents Jeff Koons? Who produced *BlacKkKlansman*? While I would argue other cultural businesses have more slightly recognizable brands—Motown, Death Row, Castelli, Miramax, etc.—the general principle remains. Audiences know artists, not the companies that produce them. And at least in the United States, it has always been this way for publishing.

Since publishing houses largely tend to go unnoticed, and because there are so few journalists who cover the publishing industry (as opposed to covering news about books and authors), many Americans are unaware of the seismic changes the industry has undergone over the past fifty years, which has been a period of intense conglomeration. Smaller publishing houses have been bought up by larger ones, who in turn have been bought up by giant houses, themselves subsidiaries of gigantic corporations. Rupert Murdoch, the owner of News Corp, owns HarperCollins, which in turn owns Ecco, which was an independent press until 1999. This kind of funnel is extremely common, and it means that the publisher of Donald Trump Jr.'s *Triggered* and Alice Sebold's *The Lovely Bones* is the same company.

Today, there are five conglomerates, known as the Big Five: Hachette, HarperCollins, Macmillan, Penguin Random House, and Simon & Schuster. For many authors, getting a "Big Five" contract is their main career aspiration. Books published by these houses generally offer the largest advances, have the biggest marketing budgets, get the most reviews and coverage, and sell the most copies. However, since these houses usually publish far more books per year than smaller presses and have more of a bottom-line profit motive, they often offer authors less individual attention, suffer from more staff turnover, and edit manuscripts too quickly or superficially.

It's a simple story of capitalism, the result of an accelerated process of mergers and acquisitions. A good analogy for the difference between conglomerate publishers and independent presses would be the difference between chains and individually owned restaurants or hotels. There are advantages and disadvantages to each, and where you stay or eat varies depending on what you are seeking. There also can be considerable variation within these two main categories: of course chain hotels and restaurants can be superior in quality, attention, and detail to some individually owned ones. Beer is another good analogy: Miller and Budweiser are the Big Five, and the numerous delicious craft breweries are independent presses.

The reputations of independent presses vary, as do the reputations of conglomerates. Some people consider indie presses to be the "minor leagues" of publishing, good for authors who are not quite ready for prime time, a farm team of talent for the big leagues. Some consider them to be superior to the conglomerates, representing the cutting edge or the avant-garde of literature. These houses, the arguments go, will produce the writers on the college syllabi of the future, while the splashier, better-paid authors of the moment will eventually be forgotten, weeded from libraries and the canon that lasts through the ages.

What I love about independent presses, and what I love about running one, is that unlike conglomerate publishers, we make business decisions that align more readily with the values of most readers. We are not trying to be all things for all people, and we're less watered-down because of it. We aren't solely driven by profit, so we're able to refuse to publish books that do not fit into our mission. We help local and national economies—we are more likely to have our books printed in the United States instead of China, for example. We are more agile, more open to experimentation, more personal. We are a hedge against an industry that has increasingly become perilously monolithic.

If independent publishers could educate the public about the differences between themselves and their conglomerate peers in the same way that independent bookstores have distinguished themselves from chain bookstores and Amazon, the reading ecosystem would be healthier. Publishers have never had a clear brand identity in the United States, but now, more than ever, would be a good time for us to learn to differentiate between the publisher of Laura Ingraham's books and the publisher of Jesmyn Ward's.

Independent booksellers, the model for independent publishers, should also be our natural allies. Indie bookstores have done a bang-up job educating the public about their value, and why customers should buy from them instead of from Amazon. To have independent publishers achieve that strong brand identity is a more difficult task, but a worthy goal nonetheless.

Say, for example, a consumer goes to a bookstore on Independent Bookstore Day (an example of the way indie bookstores ingeniously market themselves). She goes intentionally, because she understands the importance of supporting Indie Bookstore Day, the local economy, and that particular store. She decides, before she walks in, to spend about twenty dollars; the exact title she gets isn't as important as the act of buying.

It is highly unlikely that, in addition to this decision to support an independent bookstore, she will also decide to support an independent press. Say she finds three potential books to buy: two from conglomerate publishers and one from an independent press. She could look at the spine for the publisher's colophon, or logo, and choose the independent one. But how will she know which is which? Even I don't always know, based on the name of the imprint. It often requires a fair amount of googling to learn which unfamiliar imprint is owned by a multinational corporation and which is owned by a guy upstate. Perhaps independent publishers should create a sticker to let consumers know the book was published by an independent; this might persuade our consumer to choose that one from her pile.

That's what I have sought to do with Belt. If many of my decisions over the past six years have been admittedly haphazard, a lot of throwing the pasta against the fridge to see if it sticks, others have been consistent, primarily the development of a clear identity, or what we now default to calling a brand. I have always wanted our books to be noticed for the quality of the writing, the integrity of the topic, *and* the reputation of the publisher. Why can't publishing houses become more recognizable to readers, more clearly distinguished from each other? My dream has been to have a reader scan a bookstore display table, see all the books, notice one, and say, "Oh I bet this is a Belt book," then pick it up to see our cute little belt logo on the spine. We have developed a look to our books that is consistent across titles without being too matchy-matchy. We publish books that have some internal coherence in content, even now that we have expanded beyond publishing only books about the Rust Belt. We prioritize distinctive voices, intellectual rigor, and accessible prose.

Because publishing houses have never had strong brands in the United States as do, say, clothing lines or magazines or perfumes or toys or almost any other consumer product, it makes creating one seem a bit foolish. But never before has publishing become so corporate. The economic distinctions between different houses should become more recognizable, and readers should be better equipped to differentiate between types of presses. Ensuring a variety of types of publishers means protecting a healthy ecosystem for books. It is as important to distinguish and support independent presses as it is to distinguish and support independent booksellers. Booksellers are ahead of publishers in educating the public; hopefully, independent presses can learn from them and catch up.

The Big Five US Trade Book Publishers

1 PENGUIN RANDOM HOUSE

Knopf Doubleday Publishing Group
Alfred A. Knopf, Anchor Books, Doubleday, Everyman's Library, Nan A. Talese, Pantheon Books, Schocken Books, Vintage Books, Vintage Español

DK
Alpha, Dorling Kindersley, Prima

Penguin Publishing Group
Avery, Berkley, Blue Rider Press, Current, DAW, Dutton, G.P. Putnam's Sons, Pamela Dorman Books, Penguin Books, Penguin Classics, Penguin Press, Perigree, Plume, Portfolio Penguin, Riverhead, Sentinel, Tarcher, Viking

Penguin Young Readers Group
Dutton Children's Books, Dial Books for Young Readers, Firebird, Frederick Warne, G.P. Putnam's Sons for Young Readers, Grosset & Dunlap, Kathy Dawson Books, Kokila, Nancy Paulsen Books, Philomel, Price Stern Sloan, Puffin Books, Razorbill, Speak, Viking Children's Books, World of Eric Carle

Random House
Currency, Alibi, Ballantine Books, Bantam, Del Rey, Delacorte Press, Dell, Flirt, Hydra, Loveswept, Lucas Books, Modern Library, One World, Random House, Spiegel & Grau, The Dial Press, Amphoto Books, Broadway Books, Clarkson Potter, Convergent Books, Crown Archetype, Crown Business, Crown Forum, Crown Trade, Harmony Books, Hogarth, Image Catholic Books, Pam Krauss Books, Potter Craft, Potter Style, Ten Speed Press, Three Rivers Press, Tim Duggan Books, WaterBrook Multnomah, Watson-Guptill, Zinc Ink

Random House Children's Books
Alfred A. Knopf for Young Readers, Crown Books for Young Readers, Delacorte Press, Doubleday, Dragonfly Books, Ember, Golden Books, Laurel-Leaf Books, Now I'm Reading!, Random House Books for Young Readers, Schwartz & Wade, Sylvan Learning, The Princeton Review, Wendy Lamb Books, Yearling Books, Make Me a Worl

Travel / Living Language/ Audio
Books on Tape, Fodor's, Listening Library, Living Language, Penguin Audio, Random House Audio, Random House Large Print, Random House Puzzles and Games, Random House Reference

2 HARPERCOLLINS

Harper Voyager, Morrow Cookbooks, Bourbon Street Books, Broadside Books, Dey Street, HarperCollins 360

Ecco Books
Anthony Bourdain

Harper
Harper Business, Harper Design, HarperLuxe, Harper Paperbacks, Harper Perennial, Harper Wave

Harper One
Amistad, HarperElixir, HarperVia, Rayo/HarperCollins Español

HarperCollins Children's Books
Amistad (Children), Balzer & Bray, Collins, Greenwillow Books, HarperCollins e-books, HarperFestival, HarperTeen, HarperTrophy, Katherine Tegen Books

Audio
HarperAudio, HarperCollins Children's Audio

Harlequin
Carina Press, Harlequin Books, Harlequin TEEN, HQN Books, Kimani Press, MIRA Books, Worldwide Mystery, Park Row Books, Graydon House

William Morrow
Harper Voyager, Morrow Cookbooks, William Morrow Paperbacks, Witness Impulse, Avon, Avon Impulse, Avon Inspire, Avon Red

Harper Collins Christian
Grupo Nelson, Thomas Nelson, Nelson Books, Tommy Nelson, W Publishing Group, Walden Pond Press, WestBow Press, Blink , Zonderkidz, Zondervan Academic

3 MACMILLAN
Celadon Books, Flatiron Books, Macmillan Audio, St. Martin's Press, Picador

Macmillan Children's Publishing Group
Farrar, Straus & Giroux for Young Readers, Feiwel & Friends, First Second, Henry Holt Books for Young Readers, Imprint, Kingfisher, Priddy Books, Roaring Brook Press, Square Fish

Farrar, Straus and Giroux
Faber and Faber, FSG Originals, Hill and Wang, North Point Press, Sarah Crichton

Henry Holt
Holt Paperbacks, Metropolitan Books, Times Books

St.Martin's Press
Griffin, Minotaur, St. Martin's Paperbacks, Thomas Dunne Books, SMP Swerve, Wednesday Books

Tor/Forge
Forge, Orb, Starscape, Tor, Tor Teen, Tor Labs

4 SIMON & SCHUSTER

Simon & Schuster Adult Publsihing
Simon & Schuster Adult Publishing, Atria, Skybound Books, Emily Bestler Books, Enliven, Free Press, Gallery, Howard, Jeter Publishing, North Star Way, Pocket, Pocket Star, Scout Press, Scribner, Simon & Schuster (imprint), Threshold, Touchston, Avid Reader Press, Tiller Press

Simon & Schuster Children's Publishing
Beach Lane Books, Little Simon, Margaret K. McElderry, Paula Wiseman Books, Saga Press, Salaam Reads, Simon Pulse, Simon Spotlight

Simon & Schuster Audio Publishing
Pimsleur, Simon & Schuster Audio

5 HACHETTE

Grand Central Publishing Forever
Forever Yours, Twelve, Vision, Goop Press

Little, Brown and Company
Back Bay Books, Jimmy Patterson, Lee Boudreaux Books, Mulholland Books

Little, Brown and Company Books for Young Readers
LB Kids, Poppy

Hachette Nashville
Center Street, Faith Words, Jericho Books

Orbit
Redhook, Hachette Audio

Hachette Books
Black Dog & Leventhal Publishers

Perseus Books
Avalon Travel, Basic Books, Basic Civitas, Da Capo Press, Da Capo Lifelong Books, PublicAffairs, Running Press, Seal Press, Westview Press

Disney-Hyperion
Hyperion Audio, Hyperion eBooks, Hyperion East, Rick Riordan Presents, Voice

Selected Bibliography

There have been astonishingly few books published about publishing in the twenty-first century. Here are many of them. (Count the women authors, and be saddened.)

Cultural Histories:
Well-researched cultural histories of publishing written by people who were not publishers themselves—usually written by journalists or scholars—are scarce, and highly sought after!

Boris Kachka, *Hothouse: The Art of Survival and the Survival of Art at America's Most Celebrated Publishing House, Farrar, Straus and Giroux* (2014)

Loren Glass, *Rebel Publisher: Grove Press and the Revolution of the Word,* also called *Counter-Culture Colophon: Grove Press, the Evergreen Review, and the Incorporation of the Avant-Garde* (2013)

John B. Thompson, *Merchants of Culture: The Publishing Business in the Twenty-First Century* (2010)

Memoirs:
A number of former editors and publishers (all white men) have written memoirs about their experiences.

Roberto Calasso, *The Art of The Publisher* (2015)
Jason Epstein, *Book Business* (2002)
Andre Schiffrin, *The Business of Books* (2000)
Michael Korda, *Another Life* (1999)

Guidebooks, Handbooks, Resources:
These titles seek to explain the business, and are most similar to mine.

Courtney Maum, *Before and After the Book Deal: A Writer's Guide to Finishing, Publishing, Promoting, and Surviving Your First Book* (2020)
Mike Shatzkin and Robert Paris Riger, *The Book Business: What Everyone Needs to Know* (2019)
Jane Friedman, *The Business of Being A Writer* (2018)

Academic Titles:
In addition, several academic books have interesting and useful information, even for non scholarly audiences, even if not about publishing per se. These include:

Leah Price, *What We Talk About When We Talk About Books* (2019)
Dennis Duncan and Adam Smyth, *Book Parts* (2019)

CHAPTER TWO:

"I Have a Good Idea for a Book"

Deduced from my somewhat limited study of people I've met in airports and at Belt events, about 82 percent of Americans think they have a good idea for a book. Now, it's definitely a very feel-good and motivational thing to say everyone has a book in them, but I do not believe this. (I also do not think everyone has a movie in them, or a restaurant, or a surgery, or whatever other activity requiring expertise people assume they could totally do). I do think everyone has a good essay in them, though. Belt's city anthology series, books containing dozens of essays about a city, often written by people who have never published before, bears this out to a certain extent.

So when I meet people who tell me they have a book idea, and they ask me what I think about that idea—perhaps Belt would be interested?—the first question I ask is: "What else has been written on this topic lately?" Almost invariably, the person cannot answer. Even worse, they sometimes offer this dreaded response: "I don't have time to read." Often, this is uttered with great pride, followed by that wretched, perverse boast: "I'm too busy."

Think about saying this to a person whose livelihood is focused on publishing products for people to read for fun. Think about saying this to the person you might ask to spend tens of thousands of dollars to make your writing into a book. Would you apply to be a chef at a steakhouse and proudly proclaim you are too important or busy to taste red meat? Would you pitch a new type of potato chip without first going through the snack aisle to see what other kinds of chips are on the market?

Many nonwriters who are sure they have a great book idea—but (sorry to say) do not—are not thinking about their idea as one within a marketplace of other ideas. They are—and I do not mean this in a nasty way, but a technical one—thinking selfishly. They are thinking about how fascinating their grandfather who fought in World War II is, or how interesting their own divorce has been. And that's fine! It may be there is a fascinating history or memoir there. But if you have an idea for a book, the key question is not about whether a topic is interesting to you, but whether or not someone might want to spend thousands of dollars on this idea to make it into a physical object for readers. And the answer to that question lies in whether or not others might want to spend money to read it.

Writers who think selfishly aren't the kind of writers I hope to work with. I want to work with an author who has read everything that has been written on a topic, plus lots of other unrelated books, who has some sense of how those books sold and thinks, "Hmmmm, I think I have something to add to this conversation." Or maybe, "Wow, there have been four books about X recently, but they're all by men, and my take is substantially different." Or, "Everyone is writing about Y. No one is writing about the history of Y, in which I am well-versed." I want to imagine someone at a desk surrounded by recent releases who suddenly looks up and says, "Hey! There's a hole in the market for books on this topic. I can fill that gap!"

When anyone tells me they have a great idea for a book, my initial response as a publisher is always, "What else has been written on the topic?" I ask that to suss out the kind of reader the person is. Then I suggest they research the answer to consider the viability of their idea. Has it been done to death already? Does there seem to be a need for more books about the topic? How does the idea fit with similar books that have been published in the past year or two? Does it duplicate, enhance, or imitate them? Publishing is trendy, so if an idea has led to many good or best-selling books of late ("I had a breakup and decided to go hiking by myself and met so many interesting people!" or, "I grew up poor and, boy oh boy, let me tell you about the laziness of my people!"), it might find a home because a publisher figures it might do as well as those other titles. Or, the reverse might happen, and a publisher might say, "That's been done already."

In preparing to write this book, I took my own advice and found surprisingly little along the lines of a reference book about the publishing process. (Now, books about the writing process? Trust me, the world does not need any more books on that topic). The word on the street is that "books about publishing don't sell," but in my opinion, that refers more to those memoirs by end-of-career men who are reminiscing about their experiences publishing other, now-dead men. This book is not about my experiences with publishing per se; instead, it aims to describe the nuts and bolts of the publishing process as a way to make an opaque industry more transparent and understandable.

The other books about this topic that I did find included *What Editors Do: The Art and Craft of Book Editing, Getting It Published,* and *The Business of Being a Writer.* None of them are exactly like my book, so I decided there was a hole in the market. (I also discovered that the University of Chicago Press, the publisher of all three, has a monopoly on good books on this topic!)

But it's still a big risk. It may be, in fact, that "books about publishing don't sell."

Proposals

If you've decided you want to secure a traditional publisher for your nonfiction book idea, and you have found there is a need and demand for such a title, the next step is to write a proposal.

Book proposals for nonfiction have evolved into impossible beasts. They can be up to sixty pages long, and for a writer hoping for a Big Five contract sold by an agent, they can take anywhere from four months to a year to write. And that doesn't count the time for revisions that many agents will advise their clients make before sending the proposal out to editors and editorial boards.

These expectations for proposals create a few endemic problems. First and foremost, it is extremely difficult to write a serious nonfiction book proposal while you're also supporting yourself. The proposal is a job in and of itself. One friend told me she would have had to take four months off work to write a proposal strong enough to garner the advance she would need . . . to take off time from work to actually write the book. In other words, it was impossible. So even though she had lots of material for the book and a draft in process, she never even tried to get a contract for what would have been a fabulous book because she did not have time to write the proposal. I imagine some wood-lined and leather-filled room in book purgatory filled with the promise of books that were never written because the proposal process was too difficult. This is not a room the world needs.

Second, proposal writing and book writing are not the same thing. They are different genres. It's like writing a poem in order to write a play, penning a novel to make a case for a research grant, or pitching a white paper in order to paint a mural. Being good at one part of the process does not mean one will necessarily be any good at the other. As proposal expectations rise, and as authors have to work for months on something only tangentially related to writing the book itself, contracts will go to those people who are good at writing proposals. As a result, the books we get in the world will more often be written by folks like that, which will decrease the overall diversity of books that get made. The books we get may also be more formulaic because they have been laboriously outlined in advance according to the structures favored by agents and editors at the time of composition.

All of these conditions create an impoverished landscape of nonfiction overall. In the publishing industry right now, for example, one by-product of the process I've detailed above is the assumption that all nonfiction must be narrative. Narrative nonfiction is the coin of the land. It is currently so dominant that many prospective authors squeeze their ideas, topics, and habits of thinking into a story structure that does not suit them or their material. But here's the thing: there are lots of other structures for nonfiction. You can write an argument! You can proceed by association, or through a variety of case studies, or impressionistically! It's fun to consider other organizational strategies that are not primarily narrative. We should all do it more often.

Third, selling books through an extensive proposal process favors writers who work by plotting in advance. Me? I am not good at that; it's not how my mind works. I write by tinkering, by intuition, by discovering what I want to say as I draft, and then by revising over and over again. My proposals are always thin and less compelling than either my initial ideas for a book or the final product are.

The proposal process tilts nonfiction toward more formulaic books (no offense intended; this book is rather formulaic), and away from experimental ones that are difficult to outline before they have been written. When I am acquiring books for Belt Publishing, I de-emphasize the importance of tables of contents in proposals. I prefer to let the shape of the book develop as the writer drafts, tinkers, and discovers. If I have read other published writing by that author that shows dexterity with prose and structure, I can trust that they will figure out the best order for the book. "Wow, I really want to read that book" is my favorite way to respond to a proposal. I would much rather offer them a contract then, encourage them to draft away, and figure out the outline after the fact.

(Novelists are expected to write complete books before trying to get contracts, and in this sense, they are better off than nonfiction writers because there's less pressure on the proposal. But writing fiction can also require much more time, or the discipline to create time, before the author receives a contract, and, sometimes, the accompanying money that could be used to buy time to write.)

When I reach out to prospective authors to see if they have book ideas for Belt, I usually tell them not to worry about writing a full proposal. A few paragraphs that give an overview of the book is usually sufficient to start a conversation. I can tell, based upon a page or two, if an idea is tenable and marketable. I can tell, based on reading some of the writer's other published work, if their writing is good enough, appropriate for what they are proposing, and if it's the type of writing we like to publish. For some writers, this process is liberating—ideas have been floating around in their heads, but they've been intimidated by the proposal process. For others, though, a more open process like this might involve too much latitude, and they need to outline or write more before committing. (Honestly, this has not happened to me yet—everyone I talk to is just fine with a back-of-the-envelope overview and outline.) Everyone has different writing habits and processes, but that's precisely why the acquisition process should be flexible enough to accommodate a range of formats and possibilities.

The Query

Usually, the first step in securing a book contract is writing a query to an agent or an acquiring editor. The query makes the case for the book to the selected gatekeepers who might be interested in it.

A query is just a well-written email. That's it. To write a good email, you should capture the interest of the reader, explain the main point of your book, make a case for why it will sell, and explain why the particular agent or editor you're contacting might be interested in it. You should do this succinctly—500 words or less—and you should write it well. But it's not a very high bar.

However, many prospective authors—even good writers with great book ideas—send terrible queries. Many queries read as if they were written that morning, slapped together in a burst of inspiration (or procrastination). Many of them reveal that the author is too far inside her own head—the book is all about me, me, me!—and they fail to show how the query is the first step in a transaction between two parties. And some queries just aren't that great at conveying the gist of the book; admittedly, that's hard to do when you haven't written it yet!

I'm not pointing out these weaknesses to chide or dissuade people from writing queries, but to inspire them.

Remember: IT IS NOT THAT HARD TO STAND OUT IN THE INBOX OF AN EDITOR OR AGENT. YOU. JUST. NEED. TO. WRITE. ONE. REALLY. GOOD. EMAIL.

About 85 percent of gatekeeper inboxes are likely filled with queries that the agent or editor will delete after scanning them for thirty seconds. You can get to the top of the pile if you spend a little time thinking and honing your initial query. Editors and people in acquisitions love an email that grabs their attention, so spend the time making every last word count, and you can get noticed.

Here is the query I sent to secure an agent for my 2016 book, *The History and Uncertain Future of Handwriting*. Ultimately, it was an effective query because it worked. It helped me find an agent, and an editor, and a contract, and a book.

The National Archives is asking for help. They have uploaded hundreds of handwritten documents and are asking for "citizen archivists" to help them transcribe letters by Thurgood Marshall, letters of conviction by Susan B. Anthony, and cancelled checks for Abraham Lincoln's salary.

They help you decipher old scripts, offering transcription tips and tutorials. "Don't try to correct spelling mistakes," they warn. "Please be true to the document and type what you see." For help with reading handwriting, the FAQ sends you to a paleography online tutorial.

Ironically, handwriting is making a comeback in the digital age. Along with the National Archives project, several other similar crowdsourcing efforts have proven effective and popular: the New York Public Library's "What's on the Menu?" project received major media attention and a call-out by Mario Batali, and Jeremy Bentham's manuscripts are being transcribed by people who are choosing to waste their time playing with old scripts instead of *Angry Birds*.

Meanwhile, though, most of us are no longer doing much handwriting of our own. A credit card receipt here and there, a to-do list, maybe a thank you letter. But all of those traditionally scripted forms of communication have been off-loaded to keyboards as well. In elementary school classrooms, cursive writing instruction is being slowly phased out.

What does it all mean? Does the decline of handwriting as a mode of writing for most Americans signal a degradation of writing, thinking, and cognitive skills in the digital age? Or is it just another evolution in the history of writing? Behind this question lies a larger one. Should we mourn or celebrate the seismic changes in writing—from handwriting done by elementary school children to texting to how best-selling authors promote their works—wrought by the digital age?

This book raises these questions through a tour of handwriting's history, present, and future. Through visits to the Folger Shakespeare Library, the new, digital Museum of Writing in London, a course in Spenserian penmanship, third-grade classrooms, home visits with contemporary authors, and elsewhere, I go on the road to look at, learn about, and question the changing nature of writing. Handwriting has never been a neutral activity–throughout its history it has been loaded with connotations of intelligence, morality, and manners.

A work of narrative nonfiction, the book will have a broad appeal, as it interweaves personal stories, scenes from classrooms, tidbits from history, and my experiences going out to find evidence around the world, from a museum in London to a Shakespearian archive to spending a week learning Spenserian calligraphy. I tell my personal struggles as a mother navigating the education system on behalf of my handwriting-challenged son. This book has a beginning (which starts about 5,000 years ago), a middle (American schools in the early nineteenth century only taught boys, not girls, to write; cursive became more "personal" than typewriting) and an uncertain end (given the revolution in digital writing, how will we teach children how to make letters fifty—or ten—years from now?).

If the gatekeeper is interested, and thinks a book might be a good fit, she will respond by asking to see a full proposal, or to chat further, or for some evidence of some other sort of enthusiasm. You should have a full book proposal ready to go when you send a query, or you should at least plan to write one soon after the query's done. If she is uninterested, she will send a rejection. More likely, she'll simply delete your email, leaving you in that increasingly common state of online abeyance, that purgatory of wondering, "Is not responding a way to say no?" Do not let this period go on for too long without moving along. Allow two to four weeks with one follow-up. That's a fine rule of thumb in this world where there are no rules.

So: one good email. That's how most books are born!

Comparative and Competing Titles

In the first book proposal I wrote, for what would eventually become *A Skeptic's Guide to Writers' Houses*, I found it was easy to write the section about comparative and competing titles (also known as the "comp" section of a proposal). I listed three titles that had been written in the nineteenth century (so clever!). At the time, there weren't too many recent titles similar to the one I was proposing, but there had been a whole genre of similar titles which had been published a century earlier that people adored. Who could resist?

I cringe, now, imagining editors reading that section of my proposal. If I'd had an agent at the time, it never would have made it into the proposal's final version. I can just see a group of editors, leaning back at their desks, cackling with laughter. Maybe they're calling their colleagues nearby, "Hey, get a load of this! This Trubek woman put books from 1898 in her comps section!" Cue office-wide laughter.

I was not the first person who misunderstood the purpose of the comps section of a book proposal. That section is not meant to showcase books that most closely resemble the one you're writing as much as it's meant prove that there are similar titles that have been published in the past few years that sold really well. If you are going to do the "it's like X meets Y" elevator pitch, it should be, as the marketing for Stephanie Land's 2019 memoir *Maid* puts it, "*Evicted* meets *Nickel and Dimed.*"

It is not terribly clever of me to suggest that a reliance on comp titles has an overall stifling effect in publishing. Comps pressure prospective authors to imagine their creative products as spin-offs of existing ones. Why not encourage folks to write a wholly original book to which is there is no peer? Plus, comp titles, since they cater to the status quo, also cater to status quo authors. Since the majority of best-selling (and well-selling) authors still tend to be those with a foothold in the establishment, they bend white, well-educated, connected, and male. Making previous titles that sold well the benchmark for commissioning a new book helps keep the conglomerate publishing industry homogenous, its authors the most privileged.

These days, I read book proposals instead of writing them. I have a firmer grasp on what the comps section is "supposed" to include, and I also have my own preferences. I can confirm that *Evicted* was by far the most popular comp title mentioned in proposals sent to Belt Publishing in the year after its release. Quickly, it became a bit clichéd to compare one's book to

Matthew Desmond's. So proposers should now skip that one. Regardless, what I look for in a proposal's comp section is evidence of what I consider the single most important quality in a prospective author: being well-read.

It should be axiomatic, but it is so very not. In order to write a book, you should read books. Lots of them.

Book proposals are unwieldy, slightly perverse creatures. Getting them wrong can often be charming. Getting them right can often be dull. And once they're done, they're sent to quixotic individuals who all have idiosyncrasies no writer can predict. A proposal is a gamble, getting a contract is a numbers game, and publishing is an ever-shifting, profit-seeking business. The only thing any of us can do to get better at writing or reading proposals is simply to read lots and lots of books.

Finding an Agent

Finding an agent to represent your book to potential editors and publishing houses can be an intimidating prospect, but it need not be. So many aspects of the process of publishing a book are opaque and confusing—there are few clear deadlines and accomplishments to tick off your to-do list. But in that overall morass, finding an agent is a relatively straightforward process.

First, you do not need an agent to get a publishing contract. Many independent presses (including Belt) will read queries sent directly to them. All university presses, many with trade divisions, accept queries from authors. Self-publishing only requires you to represent yourself. Many successful writers, including most of Belt's best-selling authors, do not have agents.

If you are interested in receiving a larger-than-average advance, having someone knowledgeable negotiate contract terms on your behalf, or publishing with a conglomerate press, you will likely need to secure an agent.

The first step, of course, is to write that really good query email. That will tease the agent with a compelling hook, a succinct and clear explanation of what the book will contain, a bio that helps them understand why you are qualified to write and promote the book, and information about similarly published books to show you understand your book's particular niche in the larger publishing landscape. Do all that in three to five paragraphs, and you've completed the first item on the checklist.

You want to send that email to individual agents who are well-positioned to sell your idea to editors, and who may have an interest in your book's topic or an interest in you as an author. Finding these people may involve a little bit of research and legwork. Here are some potential places to look:

1) Read the acknowledgments sections in recent books that are similar to yours and look for those moments when an author mentions her agent. An agent once wrote me, "We read queries that much more carefully when an author says (plausibly), 'I see authors X and Y say good things about you, and my book I think will be of similar interest to you for these reasons.'"

2) Cast about for books similar to the one you want to write, and make a note of the books' representing agents. Follow those agents on *Publishers Marketplace*.

3) Read a variety of the many online resources and books that include interviews with agents and resources for finding agents.

Then, decide which agents you think would be interested to hear from you, and with whom you may like to work. Send them your crisp, compelling query, personalizing each one by noting the specific information you gleaned about the agent that led you to email. If your query is good, and if you are exceedingly lucky, one or more agents will be interested. They will respond in various ways, asking to see more (a sample chapter, a partial manuscript, a fuller proposal that includes marketing plans or comp titles) or to set up a phone conversation. After that, they might offer to represent you. What that means, at this point in the process, is a fairly simple contract. You are not committing to this person for life, and you can change agents much more easily than you can back out of a publishing contract.

Once an agent offers to represent you, you need to change your usual begging/hoping/crossing fingers stance toward the publishing process in general. At this point, the you become the person who's doing the interviewing, and the agent is the person who's asking to be selected. Writers should, if it all possible, be confident and maybe even a bit arrogant, even if it's all make-believe. "Tell me what you will do for me" would be a fine message to convey to a potential agent (as opposed to, "Please, please, please like me, even if it's just a little bit. I promise I won't bother you too much!"). You and the agent are forming a partnership, and both parties should feel comfortable with each other and happy about working together going forward.

So often, writers have agents, but they don't have a comfortable relationship with them, so they are too anxious to ask them difficult questions. Instead, they ask other writers. I have done this! My friends and I do it all the time! The whisper networks are epic: "Why haven't I heard from my agent in a month? Why isn't my agent telling me what that editor said when he passed on the project?"

A great relationship between a writer and agent, though, will be easy and open, and the writer will be comfortable asking questions.

Often, agents will ask the writer to make changes to a proposal before it's sent off to editors. These changes can be substantial. For example, an agent might send a novelist back to revising her manuscript for another year before she resubmits it to the agent for another look. But these changes can also be minor. The writer can choose if she wants to make these changes or not; another agent may not make the same requests, or they may have different opinions about what might make the proposal more appealing to editors. Agents are just individuals with idiosyncrasies like the rest of us. (So too are the editors to whom they will send the project.) If an agent is interested in a writer's project but wants various changes to be made, the writer should definitely feel empowered to reject those suggestions, cross that agent off her list, and move on. On the other hand, an agent may have knowledge and skill to see potential and might well compel a writer to decide to drastically retool their project. Be patient, and work with that person who is offering their expertise.

Once the proposal is in good shape, the agent will then send it to editors. It's a similar process to when the writer sent her initial query to agents, but now the agent is querying editors on the writer's behalf. Editors will pass, bid, request another sample chapter, ask if the writer would consider making a large change or two based on their interest, etc. Thankfully, there is usually an understanding between agents and editors that editors should respond in a timely fashion, so the endless waiting and silence that marks so much of the writing game doesn't come into play here.

Whether a writer should aim for the hottest agent making the biggest deals, or the newest agent looking to establish himself and who's eager for clients he can nurture for a career, is a complicated question to which there is no one right answer. It depends upon the goal of the writer. If a writer has what she thinks is a brilliant, one-shot idea that she primarily wants to do because she wants a lot of money up front, then I would suggest finding the most-connected, big-shot agent. The downside might be that that large advance may be the only money the writer ever sees for that book or any subsequent ones because expectations were so high from the jump. If a writer is seeking to establish a career from writing books and wants allies along the way, I would suggest working with an agent with whom she has the most affinity, and who seems most eager to spend time, energy, and attention on the writer. The advance for the first book would not be the most important criteria; instead, it might be finding the most talented editor, or the most imaginative house, to lay the groundwork for steady, increasingly favorable contracts in the future.

If a project sells, an agent will negotiate contract terms on your behalf and take a cut—usually 15 percent—of whatever money you receive for that project. As the intermediary between the publisher and the writer, agents are also the ones who receive payments from the publisher; they cash the checks, take out their fees, and then send the writer the remainder.

Writing the Book

Once your query has been accepted, your agent secured, and your proposal sold, you just need to write the book. Good luck with that!

CHAPTER THREE:

How Much Does It Cost to Publish a Book?

There is a common misperception among authors and aspiring authors that publishers de facto profit from their writing. This causes some righteous threads on Twitter decrying publishers' bad faith on various issues: not paying for fact-checking, not paying high enough royalties, not putting enough money into marketing, or not paying anthology contributors adequate stipends for their contributions.

It is true that publishers desire to profit from the writing of others; that is how the business works. Even nonprofit publishers have this desire, it's just that their "profits" are equal to their "overhead paid through revenue" or some other budgetary shift.

But a strange truth about publishing is that, most of the time, publishers lose money on authors' writing. The conventional wisdom is that 20 percent of the books that get published pay for the other 80 percent that lose money. Publishing executives could be on *Shark Tank* every week, pitching each title to potential investors, talking up its marketability. Each book a publisher launches is its own miniature, stand-alone start-up. Like most start-ups and small businesses, the vast majority of books "fail" in a monetary sense. Every book is a gamble. Publishing could have a game table on the floor of a Vegas casino, nestled between blackjack and roulette. Bet on which title will earn out, and which will fail. When a title doesn't break even, the casino swipes the chips off the table. But when a bet wins, it can make up for all those losses. A few bestsellers can support a press despite many money-losing titles.

So how do publishers decide which books to bet on? There's lots of risk involved when you take a look at a few words sent via email and decide that those words might, in one to three years, end up selling enough copies to earn back the money that you spent to make those words into a book, and then earn a little more so the publisher can take a little bit of money home herself.

Publishers ask two main questions, and they're the same two questions any capitalist or gambler asks: how much should we stake, and how much might we profit?

To answer those questions, most publishers do a ridiculously complicated set of projections on a profit and loss spreadsheet (P&L). This process involves guesswork into a number of different categories: how much a book will cost to print, how many copies will sell, how many ordered copies will be returned, how much the author will receive in an advance, what the list price will be, what trim size it will have, how much money it will take to market and publicize the book, whether it will be hardcover or paperback, if it will appeal to distributors who help sell the title to accounts like Amazon, Barnes & Noble, and independent booksellers. Some of these numbers are based on actual data, some are good estimates, and some are inferences based upon past experience. But most of them are magical fairy dust wishes. A P&L is basically a work of fiction, make-believe cells that tally up all the costs and revenue for a project that will not hit the market for another few years. It makes the decision to publish a book look more like a sound business plan than a gut instinct that a little ball will fall on number thirty-one on the wheel, but in truth, roulette may be a good metaphor. It's silly, really, but it's the practice of the industry.

Complex and chance-centric as they are, P&Ls provide crucial insight into the business of books. Even if they are often inaccurate or useless for publishers, they are key for anyone interested in the cogs of the industry, and those who assume publishers de facto profit from the labor of writers.

Allow me to walk you through one Belt Publishing P&L that we created to decide whether or not to publish a book called *Cleveland in 50 Maps*. I have fudged some of the numbers so I don't reveal the actual pay for various contractors, but the whole is still pretty accurate. I also chose a title that was written in-house by staff, which means there were no royalties or advances. We also entered these numbers before we had a manuscript, or a printer quote, or any of the numbers we entered into the cells. We simply guessed. Like I said, a P&L is a work of fiction.

In the top section, we entered our prospective trim size, list price, publication date, and page count for the book.

Title:	Cleveland in 50 Maps				
Author:	Crissman/Tachovsky/Wilson	Trim Size:	8x8	Advance:	$0
ISBN:	9781948742559	Retail Price:	$30.00	Print Royalty (list):	0%
Pub Date:	15-Oct 2019	Page Count:	144	Ebook Royalty (net):	0%

Then we made up some sales numbers—this was one year before the book actually went on sale. We guessed our distributor would order 2,500 copies for this book. Of those, only 1,875 would actually be sold because of the dreaded returns system (see Chapter Six). We hoped for a robust 600 copies that we would sell directly to consumers because we are based in Cleveland and have a lovely crew of fans who understand how important direct sales are to our business model. Under that number we excitedly entered zero returns. Then we added a modest number of e-book sales. (This title is heavy with graphics, and e-books are notoriously graphic unfriendly.) Usually royalties and advances would be entered here as well, but this book was a special case in that regard, and our costs were lower here as a result. You can see where we would have entered them in the column reserved for advances and royalties above.

According to this model, we would net about $42,000 in sales from this title. Eventually. There is no timeframe on this P&L; it covers the life of the book. Most sales occur in the first ninety days after publication, but a book that becomes a strong backlist title can continue to sell well, if at a slower pace, for years afterward. For Belt's cash flow purposes, we want to hit our net sales number about twelve months after publication, which is about twenty-four months after we create the initial P&L.

INCOME	TOTAL
Gross Sales-Units	3,150
Returns-Units	-625
Net Sales-Units	2,525
Gross Sales-Dollars $	$51,250
Returns-Dollars $	($9,375)
Misc. Income (rights, etc.)	
Net Sales-Dollars $	**$41,875**

But wait: that $41,875 figure isn't profit. It's simply the sales. We still need to count up our expenses, estimating what the book will cost us to make and sell.

EXPENSES	TOTAL
Print & Production	$18,500
Distribution Fees	$7,081
Royalties	$0
Unearned Advance	$0
Marketing Costs	$1,500
Other Costs	$0
Total Cost of Goods	**$27,081**

The single largest production expense for most books is printing. Paper is expensive! In our P&L, we estimated that this full-color, hardback book of 150 pages would cost $10,000 if we printed 3,000 copies, or about $3.33 per copy. This is a much higher per-unit cost than our more common 200-page paperbacks, which cost between $1 to $2 per unit. *Cleveland in 50 Maps* also had a higher retail price of $30, compared to the $16.95 we usually charge for our paperbacks. We estimated that our distributor, who helps us sell copies, would receive about $7,000 for their work on our behalf. (Remember: these are not real numbers, but accurate ballpark estimates. The amount a distributor charges a publisher cannot be revealed publicly.) We added another $1,500 to our production expenses to publicize the book—sending press releases to local media and bookstores to let them know about it and organizing events to promote and celebrate the title (see Chapter Seven).

But wait—there are more expenses! We have to pay an editor, a copyeditor, a proofreader, a cover designer, an interior designer, and others who contributed to the book. We also need to figure in the cost of securing permissions for images. If we are going to make advance copies of the book to send to media and booksellers, we also need to add in those costs, as well as the postage required to ship them.

Below, you can see the hypothetical costs for all of these components of book production. Note that the P&L doesn't include the costs of a publisher (me!), or office space, or the labor to ship copies. These are considered overhead and might be included in a flat percentage at other publishing houses. But to keep my explanation as simple as possible, I have not included those.

PRODUCTION COSTS	
Editorial	
Editing	$2,000
Copyediting	$500
Proofreading	$500
Indexing	$0
Photography/Illustrations	$500
Contributor Payments	$1,000
Design	
Cover	$500
Interior	$3,500
Typesetting	$0
TOTAL	**$8,500**

MARKETING COSTS	
Galley Printing	$0
Shipping	$0
Publicity	$1,500
Other	$0

PRINTING COSTS	
Quantity	3,000
Cost	$10,000
Unit Cost	$3.33

TOTAL UNIT COST (including Production)	
Production Cost	$8,500
Printing Cost	$10,000
Quantity	3,000
Effective Unit Cost	$6.17

Add all of those numbers together and the total projected cost to bring *Cleveland in 50 Maps* to readers is $27,081. And if all these numbers prove true, we will make a profit of $14,794, a 35 percent margin.

Again, this was all conjecture when we initially created it. Three months after this book was published, over a year or so after the P&L was created, I could already see what we got wrong. The total page count was a little lower than anticipated, but the printing costs turned out to be higher; the number of books sold through our distributor was lower than I thought they would be, but the direct sales were higher. The editorial expenses were slightly lower than we anticipated. Taken as a whole, this P&L was pretty accurate, though.

This is not always the case. Some P&L projections wildly diverge from actual P&Ls. The single key factor is sales. If we had projected we were going to sell 3,000 copies of *Cleveland in 50 Maps* and only sold 200, we would have lost money. And this often happens. As I mentioned earlier, conventional wisdom says it happens about 80 percent of the time.

But once in a while—oh, say, one out of five times—a book's sales far outstrip expectations. Books that sell far more than projected are the backbone of publishing. For example, pretend that instead of $14,000, we netted $100,000 from *Cleveland in 50 Maps*. Every title holds within it that possibility (as opposed to, say, a restaurant serving steak: it might make profit from every filet mignon it sells, but it will never sell just one steak that quadruples that profit.) And in publishing, that one jackpot can cover many bad bets.

The ability to bet more money on more books is a key difference between independent presses and conglomerate ones. Usually, a conglomerate press can bet a $100,000 advance to an author three years before a manuscript is due, and five years before the book will be published, in the hopes that it might sell enough to profit the company $1,000,000 another two years after that, when the money from sales actually comes in. If they lose the bet, they can write off that advance, and all the other expenses, as a loss. Usually, though, an independent press can neither wait that long nor risk that much money.

For authors with contracts for conglomerate houses, the advantage is that they receive more money up front. But the disadvantage, more often than not, is that failure is built into the deal—most authors will never sell enough copies to receive royalties after the book is released. With independent presses offering smaller, more realistic advances, chances increase that an author might outstrip expectations and receive royalties.

Basing all your business decisions on spreadsheets that are created years before any of the actions the numbers signify occur may not be the healthiest or most accurate method. And at Belt, we regularly make decisions based on non-P&L factors; often, we skip this step entirely. Sometimes, we publish a book because the staff thinks it would be *really fun* to do so, or it is right up our alley interest-wise, and even if we may not profit, we likely will not lose money on it. Often, we "take a flyer" on a book by an author with no platform or previous publication track record, but who writes such a compelling proposal we want to give them a chance. Other books just seem so "Belt-y"—they represent exactly why we decided to start the press—because they tell an untold regional history or because they are intellectually rigorous without being pedantic—that we have to publish them to stay true to who we are.

The Backlist

While P&Ls consume a lot of energy and hand-wringing at most publishing houses, they are not the key to success. The real secret to a successful publishing company is something much quieter, and much easier. It's also something that often escapes notice completely: the backlist.

Backlist titles are those books a house has published for at least a year, which distinguishes them from the frontlist titles, which are the recent or soon-to-be-published books. Let us return to the P&L for *Cleveland in 50 Maps* to illustrate the sneaky power of the backlist. Let's say that one year after its publication, the book has sold the 2,500 copies needed to earn a $14,000 profit. That means we would still have about 500 copies left from our original printing run of 3,000 copies. At this point, we've already paid for our printing, editorial, and production costs, so those 500 copies are pretty much pure profit. If we sell them in the year after the book's initial publication, we would receive $4,500. And say we sold another 1,000 copies in 2020 of our lead title from 2017. That would net us another $10,000. Add in the sales from a few dozen other books we published in 2014, 2016, and 2019, and suddenly there is a fair amount of cash rolling in each month.

The first copy of a book is always the most expensive. The three-thousandth or the one-millionth copy are almost free.

This passive income from the backlist is how publishing houses work. Some conglomerate imprints might receive as much as two-thirds of their annual revenue from titles published decades ago. For example, many of the expenses for FSG's Hill & Wang imprint are still covered by profits from Elie Wiesel's *Night*, a book originally published sixty years ago.

Creating a publishing company, like greenlighting a book, is tough going. Almost all the work and money must be invested before any sales ever occur. But sustaining a press that's up and running is far, far easier if one publishes books that readers want to read in the future. That's the beauty of the backlist.

How to Talk Like a Publisher

Print Run: The number of copies of a book you order from the printer, usually referring to the *initial* print run, or the wild guess you make months before a title publishes about how many books will sell. The initial print runs for Belt titles ranges from 1,000 to 10,000 copies; Big Five publisher numbers dwarf ours. Michael Wolff's *Fire and Fury* had an initial print run of 250,000 or something.

Deciding on the initial print run is an art at which I suck: I have had to order a second printing, or second print run, of a title before the publication date, based on initial orders, and I have a (secret) stash of books in the Belt office that I guessed wrong in the other direction. Publishers base their guesses on the number of books that have been preordered. This is one reason preorders are important, but they can also skew things: an author might be able to convince 300 of her very savvy friends to preorder to make the numbers look good, only to find out that there are not many more than 300 readers of her book after publication date. Another author might not be so keyed into the preorder mantra, only to find that actual strangers find and adore the book a month after publication date, causing the publisher to scramble back to the printer, and stat. Other indicators of how many copies of a book will sell: the reputation of the author, the timeliness of the topic, prepublication reviews, and tarot card readings.

Guessing the print run correctly is really only important for financial reasons. Printing has a steep economy of scale, so the more you print, the less the per-unit cost. Guess too low and you pay more than you might have; same with guessing too high. But print runs can be used for marketing purposes: *Now in its eighteenth printing!!!* Sounds so impressive, right? But no one asks how many were printed each time. And there is no industry standard. So I could do print runs of fifty, and have books go into their fiftieth printing within months. Be wary of "We can't stop going back to the printer for more copies!" claims. There is no industry assumption as to how many copies are in a print run.

Signature: My favorite! A signature refers to a group of pages, printed on both sides, that a printer will print, fold, cut, and bind. Imagine a giant piece of paper, printed with eight pages of a book on one side, and another eight on the other. The printer will fold this paper a bunch of times (and in a certain order!), then cut and trim it to the size of the book (that is, the number of inches tall and wide for each page, or "trim size"), creating groups of pages they will then gather and bind. The number of pages in a signature varies; signatures for common trim sizes are typically eight, twelve, or sixteen pages.

This cool but pretty niche printer term is very important to my daily life as the keeper-in-mind-of-the-cash-flow because signatures and money are also closely bound. When we are tweaking the final elements of a book, getting it ready to send to the printer, a question that hovers is always, "What's the nearest signature?" For instance, in the run-up to sending one of Belt's 2019 titles, *Midwest Architecture Journeys*, we had to reflow the manuscript—or rearrange the margins, words, page breaks, etc.—to make is shorter. Why? Because this glossy, heavily illustrated book was costly for us to print, and in our final version, it clocked in at 289 pages. BAD NEWS. The "nearest signature" for this book, according to the printer, was 288 pages. That meant the book could either be 288 pages or 304 pages (the signature in this case was 16 pages). It could not be 289 pages, or 301 pages, because it must have been as long as the last signature. We had two options: we could keep the file as is and add a bunch of extra blank pages at the beginning and end of the book (yes, *that's* why some books have such blank pages and others do not). This would have been less elegant *and* it would have cost us significantly more. (Paper is expensive: a 304-page book costs a lot more than a 288-page book to print.) Our other option was to make cuts to bring the book down to only 288 pages. So that's what we did.

Colophon: Okay, maybe I like this one even more than signature. It's the penguin, the little house, the belt. A colophon is the logo or brand of a publishing house. (Did you know the little house was where Candide lives?) Colophon also refers to information about the printing of the book, usually in the back of the text, and was mainly used in printings' earlier days. Colophons continue today, though: you know those weird "A Note about the Text" pages that are sometimes in the back that tell you which font was used? Those are colophons too.

CHAPTER FOUR:

The Editorial Process

When I was a graduate student, I received feedback from my professors on my seminar papers and my dissertation. As an academic, I received similar kinds of feedback on my submissions to academic journals. All of these comments took the form of paragraphs and perhaps a note or two in the margins discussing my central arguments, suggesting material I should include upon revisions, and telling me the things I got wrong. When I responded to student writing during my years as a college professor, I adopted the same habits—notes in the margins, paragraph-long comments, seemingly *ad infinitum*.

The responses that mark so much writing in college, graduate school, and scholarly publishing are a kind of feedback, but I would not describe any of it as "editing," at least as far as editing is understood in journalism and book publishing. Student papers and scholarly essays involve comments, feedback, and suggestions. But real editing is much more hands-on and much more proactive.

The first time I was edited in the way that it usually happens in the publishing industry, I was taken aback. People actually made changes to my manuscript instead of suggesting them. Instead of writing, "Perhaps reorganize this?" in the margins, they would simply move the last sentence of a paragraph to the beginning. They had no qualms altering the flow of a section or inserting an entirely new sentence. They even corrected dangling modifiers without a whiff of judgment that I had made an error in the first place.

I loved being edited this way. I still love being edited heavily and often. A good editor clarifies my points, improves my style, and forces me out of ingrained habits of syntax, tone, voice, and rhetorical form.

Not everyone is like me, though. Many writers, faced with dozens (or hundreds!) of tracked changes on their Word document can become insecure, defensive, or totally defeated. Often, it's the least experienced writers who have the most difficult time being edited. They'll sometimes bristle if another person comes in and mucks around with the work they've invested so much time and energy into. Writers who have been at it longer tend to be more amenable to making changes. But editing is a crucial part of the publishing business. It's the way the initial draft of a book turns into the well-argued, pristine, readable thing it's trying to become. And there are many different types of editing, most of which a book author will receive.

Developmental Editing

Within book publishing, there are differing terms for different types of editing, and there are differing expectations for how much editing will be done on a manuscript. Much of it depends on the quality of the draft, the culture of the press (Does it generally do heavy or light edits?), and how much pressure an editor might be under (How many books is she working on at once? How quickly does she need to turn them around?). But to boil it down to a general rule, books go through three types of editing: developmental (sometimes known as a "top edit"), line editing or copyediting (the two are sometimes conflated), and proofreading.

A developmental edit is closest to the type of feedback that is the norm in academia. A developmental or top editor considers the broadest issues of a manuscript. Is the focus clear? Does the argument need to be bolstered? Are there large topics left unmentioned, or chapters that should be added? Does the structure of the manuscript work, or should the author consider rearranging all the parts to give a work of history, for example, a thematic organization instead of a chronological one? Are the tone, voice, and style appropriate, or should those be rewritten throughout the book? Does the draft lose power in the last third, perhaps because the writer was rushing to meet a deadline? Does the manuscript need to be 20 percent shorter so it doesn't drag? Or does it need to be 30 percent longer to offer a fuller treatment of the topic?

Once the developmental editor has read the manuscript and has an approach for revision in mind, she will usually write a letter to the author outlining large-scale issues that need to be addressed. Instead of marginal comments or tracked changes, the writer receives a summary of the large changes that should be made. The writer then revises, a process that might take anywhere from a few weeks to several years—usually a few months—and turns in a revised draft. Sometimes a second or third round of developmental edits is necessary in order to turn the manuscript into what the author and editor want it to be.

Line Editing and Copyediting

Line editing is the next level "down" from developmental editing. A line editor will usually assume the manuscript's structure, tone, and focus are set, and she'll attend primarily to paragraph- and sentence-level issues. She might note a writer's tendency to repeat herself, or the fact that the author relies too heavily on the same syntactical patterns. She might point out moments when the chronology or analysis is confusing and make changes to the structure and the prose accordingly. She might make cuts if a section is dragging. She also might make word choice changes or tighten the prose on the sentence level. She is making many changes, but in order to elevate the vision the author has for the book, not the vision of the editor. Like line editing, copyediting (or copy-editing, or copy editing, depending on your copyeditor / copy-editor / copy editor), involves working through the manuscript on yet another "smaller" level, this time primarily at the sentence level. The copyeditor combs through the manuscript, corrects grammar and punctuation, suggests changes in word choice and syntax, and checks for factual accuracy. She also sometimes puts together a style sheet outlining all the major changes she's made, so that the writer will abide by the new style guidelines as she continues working on the book. In some cases, the copyeditor will suggest larger changes to structure and form if there seem to be inconsistencies or if she believes they're merited. Copyeditors use a variety of guides to make decisions: *The Chicago Manual of Style* and AP are two common ones; there also may be in-house style guides. Authors often balk at changes made by a copyeditor due to their familiarity with a different style guide than the one the publisher uses, or because she does not understand an uncommon change. As long as a publisher hires an experienced, good copyeditor, I always suggest that the author trust all the changes. It is a wonderful luxury to have a good copyeditor work on your manuscript. (I accepted all the numerous changes my copyeditor made to this chapter!)

Proofreading

The last level of editing, proofreading, is usually done after the book has been typeset or laid out (see Chapter Five). It's the final check to make sure there are no errors. The proofreader gives another pass to some of the things the copyeditor has looked at already—grammar, punctuation, spelling, capitalization, and factual accuracy—to double-check that everything looks good. She also checks new sections of the book that have been added by the typesetter, including chapter headings, margins, page numbers, the copyright page, and the back cover copy.

The Proofreader's Mindset

At Belt, I know myself well enough to stay away from proofreading. I may know the rules, but I am not fastidious. Plus, I revise and edit as I proofread, which is a terrible thing to do because it requires constantly starting over again and proofing new changes. That will never produce pristine copy.

Whenever we can, Belt asks Michael Jauchen to take the last look at a manuscript. Here's his take on why he enjoys proofreading and what it's all about:

> It's largely a matter of mindset. Proofreading is its own particular kind of reading—much slower, much more technical, more machine-like. You know how Microsoft Word will allow you to show formatting marks, which reveals all the pilcrows and leader marks in a document? To me, proofreading is kind of like looking at a text in a similar way. Every single mark on the page (and even every single empty space) has to be looked at and scrutinized. When I proofread, I usually blow up the text to about 250 percent of its original size, which helps me look at it microscopically.
>
> For me, there's a genuine pleasure that comes from looking at a manuscript so microscopically, to be the person who considers every comma, every dash, every apostrophe, every word, and ensures that everything is in its proper place. In that sense, I think proofreading appeals to my own personal sensibilities—I'm hardwired as a person who likes order, organizing, process, and logistics. Proofreading has also always been a great way for me

to immerse myself and learn (and enjoy!) the richness and complexity of language—the specific and tiny ways that an incredible amount of complex meaning can be conveyed just through black marks and blank space on the page. That's still kind of magical to me every time I think about it. And being part of the process of making that meaning as clear as possible to a reader is really satisfying. I had a writing teacher once who always talked about giving your ideas a "clean vehicle" when you're writing. What she was getting at was the drive all writers have to express themselves exactly—to put the right words in the exact right order. That goes for the things writers and developmental editors do in the early stages of creating a book, but it also goes for what copyeditors and proofreaders do. It's about getting things so perfect and so right that the author's original thinking can be communicated with absolute clarity and exactness. My ultimate goal in proofreading any manuscript is to make it so perfect that the reader has no idea that I've been there at all. If I'm doing my job correctly, I completely disappear.

Here is an example of Michael's proofread pages:

And if you're looking to make life easier for your copyeditor and proofreader, here are the suggestions Michael had for writers:

Stripping the manuscript of formatting before you submit a manuscript to an editor is good advice. Having the text in a normal, consistent font with a normal consistent style just makes the read-through cleaner and easier. Also, anything you can do on your own to aim for consistency across the manuscript is really helpful to a proofreader. For example, if you have section breaks in your manuscript, don't signify those with a # sign in one chapter and *** in another. When stuff like that gets to my desk, that causes me to wonder if you were trying to signify different things with those different signs. Speaking of consistency, use the name you'd like to go by professionally in every instance in the manuscript. Title page, bio, etc. Make sure it's the same name. Also, one space after a period. Also, to anyone who still does this (for whatever reason), stop using the Enter key as a carriage return unless you're starting a new paragraph. Also, stop using the space bar to indent your paragraphs or block quotes. Also, serial commas forever.

Fact-checking

Fact-checking has become a *cri de coeur* of late. In Anand Giridharadas's savage review of *Upheaval* by Jared Diamond, he mentions the many errors that appear in the book:

> There is also a systemic issue here. The time has come for those of us who work in book-length nonfiction to insist that professional fact-checking become as inalienable from publishing as publicity, marketing, and jacket design—and at the publisher's expense rather than as a cost passed on to the author, who, understandably, will often choose to spend her money on health care. In the age of tweets, it cannot be the fate of the book to become ever more

tweetlike—maybe factual, maybe whatever. The book must stand apart, must stand above.

Others have been similarly vocal; many have taken to Twitter to discuss how imperative it is for publishers to hire fact-checkers and underwrite the expense. They receive a scad of retweets and plenty of replies endorsing the view with a simple, "This!"

I believe books should contain only correct information and "real" facts. Also, I agree that the errors found in books by Naomi Wolf, Jill Abramson, Jared Diamond, and others are serious and concerning. I also firmly believe all books should be fastidiously copyedited and proofread.

But I disagree with those who are calling out publishers for not fact-checking. Fact-checking is almost always the contractual responsibility of the writer for reasons I discuss below. But also: publishers have traditionally checked facts in manuscripts, if not fact-checked per se, during the copyediting and proofreading process.

The term "fact-checking" refers to a very specific activity involving re-researching and re-reporting everything an author has written. Say you have written a book on fifteenth-century scribes. A full-on fact-checker would need to track down and verify every statement about every scribe in the book. Was that monk born in 1487 or 1488? Did he write on parchment as the book describes or was it actually vellum? Did he always sit in a chair or did he sometimes write standing up? Basically, a fact-checker redoes every last bit of reading, interviewing, and research the author did. For newspapers, fact-checking is usually simpler, as stories are shorter and more timely than they are for much nonfiction, which often requires years of research.

A good copyeditor will do some of the same things: she will double-check birth dates and the spelling of names. A good proofreader will then do it again, checking the most obvious "facts" in a manuscript. In this sense, publishers do, or at least they should, check facts. The errors in Jared Diamond's book definitely should have been caught by the publishers. Also, if a book is extremely timely and controversial—something on the impeachment report or Trump's tax returns, for example—it would behoove any publisher to have it fact-checked as that term is traditionally defined.

But publishers do not do the same "fact-checking" work that magazines and newspapers might do. In fact, most traditional publishing contracts require authors to do their own fact-checking, or checking of facts, and will include something similar to the clause below in which authors agree, when they sign, that they are responsible for the veracity of their work:

---

4.   Warranty and Indemnification

(a)   Author warrants with respect to the Work that the Author is the sole author of the Work and that Author is the legal proprietor of all rights herein granted and has the full power to enter into this Agreement, that the Work has not previously been published except for any material expressly permitted or cleared pursuant to paragraph 3, is original, free of any lien, claim or debt of any kind, that the Work contains no matter that the publication or sale of which violates any federal or state statute or regulation, nor is it in any other manner unlawful, and that, as submitted, the Work will not violate any statutory or other copyright or any other right of third parties (including right of privacy and right of publicity), or be libelous or obscene, or in any way illegal, that all material in the Work presented as fact is true or based on diligent research for accuracy, and that any recipe, formula or instruction contained in the Work is not injurious to the user.

Much of the confusion and uproar about fact-checking books, and who should pay for it, stems from a categorical difference between publishing and journalism. Journalists are not contractually in the same relationship to magazines and newspapers as authors are to publishers. Some confusion has arisen from this difference. When a magazine publishes an article by a writer, the magazine takes responsibility for the veracity of the piece on behalf of the writer. When a publisher publishes a book, on the other hand, the author assumes responsibility.

Why the difference? Authors and staff writers have different relationships to their parent organizations. To explain, recall that most publishing houses are relatively anonymous. Readers are likely to know the author of a favorite book ("Salinger!"), but they rarely know the book's publisher. Within the world of journalism, this dynamic is reversed. Most people will remember they read an article in the *New York Times* or *NPR*; fewer will remember the byline.

This dynamic trickles down (or up) to the contractual relationships writers have with their publishers in the two industries. The *New York Times* hires staff writers and freelancers, and they do not require reporters to sign contracts taking legal responsibility for the accuracy of their articles because the newspaper's reputation rests on accuracy. So the *Times* pays employees to write articles, and the organization assumes responsibility for those employees. If a reporter makes a mistake, the fault lies with the paper itself (though, of course, the reporter may get in trouble or be fired).

Authors of books, on the other hand, have always been part of the gig economy. A book publisher does not employ authors; it hires them as independent contractors. Because of that relationship, the publisher asks the contractor to sign a legal document pledging that their work is "true or based on diligent research for accuracy." If there is an error in a book, it is the author, not the publisher, who violated the contract (though it certainly doesn't look good for the publisher either!).

None of this means anyone should be okay with having errors printed in books, of course. And it may be that the usual legal relationships and contracts between publisher and author should change. But it also might be that the dream of facticity is one that has never been realized and is itself a very modern invention.

How to Talk Fancy to Your Editor

Front Matter and Back Matter: These are elements of a book not usually included in the manuscript. They include, in the front, "matter" such as the copyright page, the half-title page, the title page, epigraph, and dedication. In the back, it usually refers to acknowledgments, author bio, bibliography, or notes. We often add the front and back matter to a book after a manuscript has been proofed, so if you want to play "find the typo!" read the front and back matter carefully. And then please do not email us to tell us what you have discovered until we are ready to send the book to the printer for a second print run, when we can make changes. Otherwise we will just have to live with those pits in our stomachs. Thanks!

Bug, Glyph: Here's how a conversation goes between editors and designers at Belt Publishing, discussing our city anthologies, in which we try to design some cool city-specific logo to use as section breaks.

"What should we use for the little thingy?"

"Um, Anne, the little thingy?"

"You know, the doodad that we put inside essays. The squiggle. The squib."

Apparently these should be called bugs, or a glyph. They are cute. For our Milwaukee anthology we used the botanical garden domes; for St. Louis, the arch; and for Akron, the Goodyear Blimp.

Stet: Stet is a proofreading term. It tells the reader to disregard the change that a previous editor or proofreader has marked (equivalent to not accepting a change in Word's track changes). The term comes from the latin verb *sto* and means "Let it stand." One of my favorite/most abhorred phrases to use is, "He stetted back all my changes!" It is my favorite because it sounds so impressive. It is abhorred because it usually means I am working with either an extremely particular or overly arrogant writer.

CHAPTER FIVE:

The Production Process

A book is so much more than the words inside it. And after the proposing, selling, drafting, and editing, a book must have a cover, an interior design, a copyright page, back cover copy, and a way for it to be sorted and catalogued so readers can find it.

Cover Design

The splashiest phase of this production process is the cover design. Covers often follow trends. Think about midcentury pulp fiction, full of gaudy, lusty images of women, or the more recent trend of stark "Big Think" books like those by Malcolm Gladwell that are mostly text against a white background, or the flurry of books featuring women looking sideways or behind them that many literary novels featured a few years ago. The past few years have seen the rise of "Instagram-friendly" designs. Many have some sort of patterned background, fronted by a blocky title font. The covers of two recent best-selling novels, *Where the Crawdads Sing* by Delia Owens and *American Dirt* by Jeanine Cummins, are good examples. It makes sense: most people choose books from images on screens, not from seeing the spines on shelves. But it is not a particularly organic way to visually represent the contents of a book.

I have been a book collector for years. Well, not exactly a collector: I'm not good at keeping valuable books in, um, valuable condition, so I am really more a book *scout*. I scour thrift stores and flea markets for books and then sell them online to real collectors who don't let dust invade the top spine. It's a fun and somewhat profitable hobby. For instance, recently I went into an Alvin Lustig rabbit hole, and both read about and bought copies of this midcentury designer's covers for New Directions' New Classics series. (The cover of this book is inspired by Lustig.) My fascination with design-forward reprint series goes way back—I also "collect" early Penguin paperbacks and the Modern Library series, and we used those exemplars to create a cohesive aesthetic for Belt's own reprint series, Belt Revivals.

According to industry wisdom, however, Belt should be less focused on design per se and more on BIG TEXT that can be easily "read" in small pixelated JPEGs. In a great article on the current book design aesthetic, Margot Boyer-Dry writes:

> At a time when half of all book purchases in the U.S. are made on Amazon—and many of those on mobile—the first job of a book cover, after gesturing at the content inside, is to look great in miniature. That means that where fine details once thrived, splashy prints have taken over, grounding text that's sturdy enough to be deciphered on screens ranging from medium to miniscule.

I get the importance of thumbnail-friendly book covers, but considering the aesthetics of a cover and the design of a book—including trim size, paper stock, the typeface used in the interior, and the size of margins—are integral parts of book publishing, and, honestly, quite fun to play around with and consider how to do best, even if it won't come across as well on Instagram, dammit. Not to mention books are in some respects a way to opt out of the internet and social media—not in defiance, but in contrast, as in, "Oh hey I just spent eight hours staring at a screen, I think I'll take a bath and read a book."

The aesthetics of a material book are an important part of design and design history, and I hope to help create books that someone might want to stare at, while finding a used copy in a thrift store in a decade or so, and think: "what a beautiful cover."

The Cover Designer's Mindset

Belt's creative director, David Wilson, is responsible for most of our covers. Here's what he has to say about his process:

> For me, the most interesting part about designing a cover is juggling all the variables—content and feeling, audience, style, design principles—to come up with a final solution. The first thing I like to know is what the book is about. Is it about mental health in the Midwest? Whiskey in Pittsburgh? Tarot and nature in the Midwest? Usually, there is a deeper layer of content to every manuscript. What does the content actually mean? Sure the book is about tarot cards and select species of animals, but the book is meant to show the reader how beautiful, magical, exotic, and attainable the world is right under our feet in the Midwest if only we stopped for a moment to look. If I know what a book means to the writer or is supposed to mean to the reader, I can begin to answer how the book cover should make the audience feel.
>
> Then I factor in the audience. The tarot book audience might be different than the whiskey book one. Usually narrowing it down to some sort of demographic helps lead the way and throws up guidelines or restrictions. I'm a fan of restrictions. Sometimes when the job is too open, things can get lost or go off the tracks. Too many directions, no clear solutions. I like bringing in restrictions to help focus the ideas and directions down.

After I gather as much information as I can on the subject, I start the design process and create concepts. I turn in super sketchy concept ideas (fig. a). They're less layouts or mock-ups and more, "Here's what I think should go on the cover, not how it should go on the cover." The editor and I go back and forth trying to whittle down our ideas to a couple winners (fig. b). After that I start thumbnails (fig. c). From there we narrow down to a final direction and I move to a "final." Usually the final needs revisions, but by this point we know where we are headed: most changes at this point are to color or font size.

This process is done hand in hand with the editor/publisher. They know their audience better than me, and having another set of eyes has always proven to be positive. Sometimes there can be too many cooks in the kitchen, but if it's one to three people, it's usually smooth and ideas come and go, building on each other for the better. The editors have toiled over the manuscript, had meetings with the author, and understand the book better than I ever could. They are my connection to what the book is and how it should feel, which to me are the most important elements in designing a cover.

The editor and I go back on forth on what's working, what's not, and sometimes we get input from the author or other parties. Then I refine the design, colors, typography, and we have a final cover.

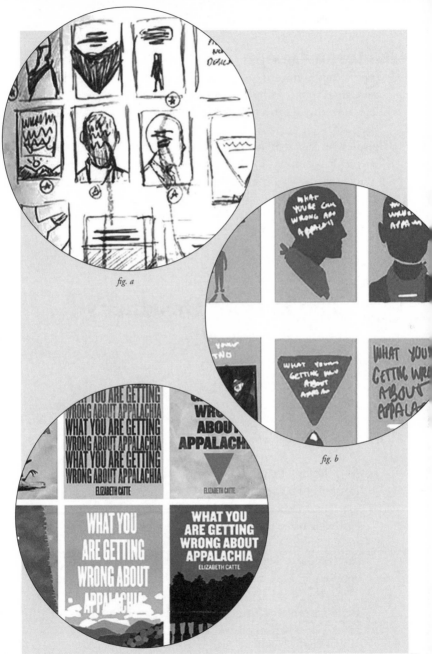

fig. a

fig. b

fig. c

Interior Design

Typesetting is the part of production that remains the most mysterious to me. So rather than try to talk about it myself, I'll defer immediately to a true expert. Creative Director Meredith Pangrace often mentions issues in manuscripts that cause extra hurdles for her that to me, someone used to working with Microsoft Word, not InDesign, are surprising. I often pretend I know exactly what she's referring to when she tells me a new sentence would require her to "reflow everything." Finally, I sat down with her, admitted my ignorance, and asked her to walk me through her job.

The Interior Designer's Mindset

"This is so boring!" Meredith kept saying to me as I asked her questions about the actions she takes after an editor sends her a manuscript and before she sends a PDF back as a first-round mock-up. But then she opened up about the process:

It's a beautiful thing to create a well-designed page, to open a book and have the words and spaces work together. I get a creative satisfaction with working with less, with black and white letters on a page. It is very meditative. It's a mathematical sort of creativity to get the letters and paragraphs to line up, a chapter to start where you want it. It is very structured, which is satisfying.

Before I touch the document I have to know how many pages it is, the trim size, and if we are using a previously designed template or a new one. Then I set up the document in Adobe InDesign. I have to make a lot of choices at the beginning about the size of the margins, which font to use, font size, what spacing to have, what the paragraph indents will be, and how to start each chapter. I also have to decide on running heads and where the page numbers will go. The front matter I save until later.

Then I take four to five pages of the document and dump it into the file I have set up with all of the above, and print it out to see how it looks. There is a disconnect between what a document looks like on screen and how it looks on a printed page; you really have to print it out to understand.

Margins are important. If you are doing a self-published book that will be uploaded to Ingram Spark or CreateSpace, they will reject the file if you don't have proper margins. Also, the margins of the left and right side of the spread (recto/verso) are different because of the gutter. The inner margin has to be wider than the outer one. You can't just think about single pages when designing and typesetting; you always have to think about it as a spread, two pages facing each other. Editors often forget this!

I have to set up the template—the set of decisions I have made about margins, paragraphs, chapter style, etc.—extremely carefully. After I have reviewed those first four to five pages, and like them, and am sure I have all the settings correct, I flow the whole manuscript in. If I've done it correctly, it will create left and right pages for the entire document.

Then I go through every single page. I decide how to style chapter headings. I decide if we want drop caps. Do we want chapters to always start on the left side? Or right? Do subsections always start on a new page? Each book is different. I go through the manuscript looking for widows—one word on one line—and any bad breaks. For instance, you usually don't want to start a new paragraph with the last line on a page.

It's like magic; it's like doing puzzles. I can hit one key and make everything change. I use kerning to make tiny changes that few would notice but that make the page look better—for instance, to make a paragraph not bleed over to the next page, I might change the kerning. Or to keep the length of a book to a signature. Sometimes, the proofreader will notice, and tell me I've tracked things too tightly.

You can never be sure that formatting will come through in the transition between, say, a Word document and InDesign. I have to check everything. Sometimes italics don't make it through the transition. Sometimes a block quote will mistakenly go on for thirty pages, and I have to go back and change everything. Section breaks often don't come through. Apostrophes and quotation marks have to be checked carefully. Tabs and blank spaces have to be checked manually.

Her final suggestions to authors?

Show your designer a book that you think looks beautiful. Help them understand the look you would like for your book. Oh, and learn how to use em dashes! And get rid of double hard returns between paragraphs.

How to Impress Your Designer

Gutter: The inside margin of a page. Gutters become very important when one of the *many* authors-to-be, new designers, and overexcited editors decide to do that thing I hate: *add images.* Images are complicated in books! The web has made us forget this! Open up the book closest to you, one without a broken binding, to the middle. Notice how it's harder to open it all the way? Now imagine someone had decided to put a picture there. Or even worse, an image that spreads across two pages. That's right, the center of the two-page-spread image would be sucked down into the binding. Never forget the gutter.

Bleed: When you use images, consider the bleed as well the gutter—it's a murder scene over there in the typesetting alley. A bleed is an image that extends to the edge of a page. A full bleed is an image that extends to the all the edges of a page. Gutters and alleys and margins all have to be carefully adjusted so the printer doesn't trim off part of the image when binding. Images, they are hard.

Drop cap: Drop caps are larger first letters of a chapter or section that extend more than one line. Drop caps are older than printed books. Even before Gutenberg, scribes would use them. Those very elaborate illustrated first letters of words in chapters in manuscripts, inculabula, and codices are drop caps. Their genesis is practical. Until the late Middle Ages, reading was noisy: people read out loud; the words were written as scripts to be enunciated, not individual words to be scanned. There were no spaces between words, and no punctuation, and no difference between capital and lowercase letters (or, to be historically accurate, majuscule and minuscule) because the reader was speaking the words aloud to himself. Large initial letters to start sections or chapters were the only marker for readers, telling them to take a breath and shift gears, as a new topic was to begin. Eventually, silent reading became the norm, and other devices developed to help readers navigate a text, such as punctuation, spaces, and, after printing, standardized spelling. Drop caps are a lovely vestige of early manuscript culture.

Bulk up the spine: I used this in conversation *without trying* the other day and I was really proud of myself. I was talking with editor Dan Crissman about our book *Cleveland in 50 Maps*, which is about 110 pages. We were talking about what kind of paper we would choose for it, and he mentioned he thought a thick glossy stock would work best. I said, "Plus it would bulk up the spine," and then gave myself a round of applause for sounding so fancy. A short book will have a thin spine—and sometimes a very thin spine is not a good thing: thin spines get lost on shelves, and it's hard to print the title and author on less than a half-inch of space. So you can use thicker paper—or wider margins, or blank pages between chapters, or other tricks you remember from college when your research paper was short of the minimum page requirement—to bulk up the spine.

Printing

At one point in time, publishing and printing were coterminous industries. They're not anymore. Printing is a complex industry of its own, and publishing houses contract with other companies who own the actual presses.

There are a variety of choices a publisher must make about how to print a book: the quality of the paper, the type of boards to use for a hardback, the type of lamination, the type of binding (perfect bound or saddle stitch), the dust jacket, and the flaps. Each choice costs a different amount, and that cost varies from printer to printer. Even paper itself can be a complex aspect of printing. Its costs vary—based on economic and other factors—with some paper stock becoming scarcer or more expensive at different times of the year. Choosing which printer to produce a book is no less complicated. Many conglomerate publishers hire Chinese companies, whose costs are lower. Belt, and many other independent presses, on the other hand, insist on working with printers based in the US.

Printing is such a fascinating and little-known facet of publishing that it could merit its own book-length guide: *So You Want to Print a Book?* For our purposes, however, the most important aspects of printing to understand are economy of scale and the different types of printing presses.

Offset printing, which uses plates to transfer text onto paper and produces the highest quality, operates on a steep economy of scale. Printing fifty copies of a 250-page paperback might cost $5 per book, whereas printing 500 copies of that same book might cost $2 per copy. Deciding on the initial print run for a book requires a set of financial projections. If you print a lot, you'll save on each copy, but you'll risk paying for books that might sit in a warehouse for years. Print too few, and you'll kick yourself for overspending.

Printing is about 30 percent of Belt's overall budget, our single highest expense after labor, so deciding how many copies of a book to print months before there is any available sales information can be stressful.

Publishers are increasingly doing an end run around this tricky decision by using print-on-demand (or POD) services. Instead of ordering thousands of books from a traditional printer, they use services that print copies upon receiving orders. The per unit cost is much higher, but there is less financial risk.

The quality of POD books has improved greatly over the past few years; the clunky amateurish versions that first hit the market have been supplanted by books that are largely indistinguishable from those from a traditional printer. Most people have probably purchased and read a POD book and have not noticed a difference in quality of paper or design. In fact, many publishers have moved their entire backlist to POD. Others, with bestsellers moving too fast for the traditional printer to keep up with demand, use PODs as a stopgap measure to keep copies flowing until the next offset printing arrives. The price of POD copies has decreased as quality has increased as well. If an offset print run might cost you $1 per unit, a POD copy might be as low as $2. That's double the price, but depending on the math you are doing (the retail price, the number of copies you anticipate selling), it might be the sensible choice.

However, the POD industry, which is rapidly shifting, is still less reliable than offset printing overall. Now that publishers are using them more frequently—and conglomeration means there are now only a few huge players in the field—there are fewer POD companies to choose from, and new quality problems are becoming more common. In its early days, the quality control worry with PODs was that they would look unprofessional. Now, PODs often look fine on the outside, but they frequently contain glaring errors on the interior. For example, page 118 might be completely smudged, or pages might haphazardly show up out of sequence. With POD, there are fewer eyes checking a book as it goes through the printing process, and major printing errors—which happen often, but are usually caught when one uses a traditional printer—often remain unnoticed until a reader opens her copy.

Using POD also means pouring more money toward the corporations that operate them (Amazon and Ingram are the two major players currently). This threatens the sustainability of local printers. At Belt, we use both offset printing and POD. POD is essential when we have printed too few copies of a book and are suddenly out of stock; it takes three to six weeks for an offset printer to send us a new printing, but only three to six hours for POD to start fulfilling orders. We simply cannot afford to lose the sales that would be cancelled if a book was even temporarily out of stock. We also use POD when an older title has sold through its print run and is selling only, say, ten to one hundred copies per year. It would tie up too much of our cash to do a new printing of that title, as it would take years for us to sell them all. Many university presses and small presses who often print less than 500 copies of a book rely on POD for the same reason.

For offset printing, by far the vast majority of the printing we do, we only work with printers in our region. Many large publishers have their books printed in China because it is cheaper; we have thus far been able to restrict our printers to those in Wisconsin, Illinois, and Michigan.

One theme that has emerged as all of publishing becomes more consolidated—not just publishers but also booksellers (Amazon) and printers (POD companies owned by Amazon and Ingram)—is, well, complexity. One cannot simply "oppose" Amazon, as it also enables smaller presses and individuals access to the marketplace they were previously prevented from or faced huge hurdles to entering. The Amazon Advantage program allowed us to distribute our books when we were too small to attract more established distributors in the publishing industry; CreateSpace allows self-publishing authors to find audiences. PODs, politically and aesthetically, are a gray area: their accessibility and democratizing power enables the work of independent presses and self-publishers, but it is reliant on an economic model that is unfavorable to those same entities.

How to Talk Dirty to Your Printer

Trim Size: This refers to the size of the book. Go to your bookshelves and notice the variety of heights and widths. Some trim sizes are fairly standard and will cost you less to print. Lesser-used ones will require more specialized equipment, paper, etc. from the printer and will be more expensive. Choose your trim size wisely! It's something I keep forgetting myself, as a publisher, until the printer quotes come in. And it's something that the self-publishing clients we work with almost never consider until we ask. Trim size is a really obvious, yet often strangely overlooked, step in creating a print-and-paper book out of pixels on a laptop.

Strip-and-Bind. I have never used this one at work, but it's probably the best one (?) to work into cocktail party chatter (?!). Strip-and-bind refers to the practice of removing the interior pages of a book from its hardcover shell—leaving just the text block—and then rebinding it to a new soft or paperback cover. Sadly, this exciting term is usually only used in depressing circumstances: the publisher, having printed more hardcover copies than she can sell, has decided to convert some of the excess inventory into paperbacks.

CHAPTER SIX:

Middlemen

Distribution, like so much else in publishing, is more complex than it needs to be. It's also far more important to the industry than most outsiders realize. Distributors are the middlemen between the publisher of a book and its seller. At Belt, we send our finished copies of books to distributors, and they in turn send those books to stores when orders are placed. Distributors also help sell titles; a fleet of salespeople fan out across the country, pitching their publishers' books to buyers at Costco, Hudson News, independent booksellers, museums, educational institutions, and wherever else books are sold.

For these services, the publisher pays a fee, giving the distributor a cut of the book sales. The larger a company is, the smaller its distributor fees. Larger independent presses can negotiate more favorable distribution contracts, and corporate publishers are large enough to have their own distribution arms.

That is how the relationship between publishers and distributors works. On the other side of the equation—from the distributor to the bookseller—the same sort of calculus prevails. Distributors offer differing discounts. For example, Amazon is often able to leverage a more favorable discount than independent bookstores can, so Amazon pays less for the books it orders than do mom-and-pop shops.

Let's say that Small Town Bookstore orders one copy of a book from Belt's distributor on January 1. The book retails for $20. Small Town Bookstore is invoiced for $10 (let's assume a 50 percent discount for this hypothetical scenario), and the distributor ships the book to them.

The distributor, then, has received $10 for this title. They take out their fee—let's say the fee is 25 percent, or $2.50. They then pay us the remainder: $7.50. (Distributors charge other fees for shipping and advertising as well, so the total that comes to us is actually closer to $7.) Whether or not we actually ever receive that money, though, is uncertain, because of the return system. If we do receive it, it will arrive in 90 to 120 days because distributors pay us about three months after an order has been shipped.

So on May 5, we will receive $7 for a copy that was ordered on January 1 and that sold for $20. Of that $7, the author receives a cut, either already paid by us with an advance, or in royalties if the advance has already earned out. Let's say that cut is 10 percent of the retail price, or $2.

With the five remaining dollars, Belt pays for printing and labor (editors, designers, publicists, and, well, me, the publisher), overhead (rent, utilities), and other business expenses.

This explanation of what, when, and how much we receive for the majority of the books we sell explains the single most important aspect of Belt's business model: our online store. For every book Belt sells directly to consumers, we receive 100 percent of what the consumer pays (minus the small costs for web hosting). And we receive it immediately. In 2018, we sold at least ten times more books, in volume, through our distributor than through our store, but we earned about the same amount from each method.

For the first few years of Belt's existence, I tried to resist outside distribution. For a while, we distributed all our books ourselves, sending orders to Amazon, fulfilling library requests individually, and spending a lot of time going to the post office. We made a greater percentage profit than than we do now, but the total number of books we sold was smaller.

Books are inexpensive and portable. Those are their greatest features, and this is the primary reason they've outlasted so many technological revolutions. The codex is simply hard to beat when it comes to a "platform" or a technology or a form used to distribute the written word to as many people as possible. And with the internet, books became even more accessible because people don't have to travel to a market—a bookstore, a library—to access one.

From the sixteenth century until about twenty years ago, the easiest way to get books to readers looked like this:

Printer →Publisher→Distributor→Bookseller/Library→Reader

Now the cycle *could* look like this (and does when people and booksellers order directly from the publisher):

Printer →Publisher→Reader

The many intermediaries between publisher and reader strip books of some of this beauty. They also make a much bigger environmental impact. Our books are shipped at least three times when they are purchased anywhere other than through direct orders to our store. Not only do they go from the printer to the distributor to the bookseller, but our distributor also has five warehouses, and they are often transferring our books from one to the other. That adds up to a large number of trucks transporting cartons of books from one intermediary to the next.

My criticism of the distribution system in publishing is theoretical, and it's not pointed toward the good folks who work in these intermediary companies today. Bookstores, like museums, are invaluable resources. They create a form—the form of an exhibit, the way books look in a store display at any one time. From the raw products of publishers, they create a lens—a narrative about books—for free to any potential reader. Unlike libraries, whose role is comprehension more than curation, booksellers discriminate and gatekeep, narrowing our choices for us, just as a museum curator chooses how paintings should be arranged to create an overall effect. We need good bookstores to help us access books like we need museums to help us access art.

But independent bookstores order from the same distributors who require publishers to publish on Amazon and who add an extra step or two between the publisher and reader. Those steps are resource-hungry, which costs publishers, costs booksellers, and ultimately costs consumers.

Amazon

First, let me start by saying that by and large Amazon is, yes, evil. I try not to buy anything from them. And yes, they hurt the publishing business.

But I concede that it is impossible to absent oneself completely from Amazon in the United States, just as it is impossible not to be capitalist in a capitalist country. Amazon owns so many oft-hidden parts of our day-to-day lives it would require enormous effort to be "Amazon-free": their cloud services through AWS, Amazon Web Services, are the back end of so much else on the web, for instance. Amazon also makes life easier and more affordable for millions of people who are housebound or who lack mobility. Finally, Belt Publishing would not exist without Amazon.

Amazon has a program called Amazon Advantage, which allows publishers to list their books on the site without having a conventional distributor. When I first started Belt, we were too small to attract a distributor, but we were able to use this program to list and sell our books on Amazon. Almost 50 percent of books sold are purchased there. Before Amazon, small presses and self-publishers (there were far fewer of them then;

Amazon also allowed much of self-publishing to exist) were not able to reach consumers so easily. Amazon is now, for better or worse, the card catalog. It is the easiest and most commonly used reference source for editors, writers, and readers, sure, but also often for researchers, librarians, bookstores, academics, and book reviewers. It functions like the Library of Congress. To not be on Amazon is a serious problem; to not be on Amazon is to lack credibility. Imagine if they did not have a program to allow smaller presses to list their titles. Then one retail book monopoly, Amazon, could create conditions that would allow Big Five publishing to further squeeze out the rest. Access to Amazon is necessary oxygen.

Let's look at it another way. Say you were a publisher who could only bind books by taking them to Kinkos and having them put one of those plastic sliding doohickeys on to secure the pages. Or let's say you could only use Comic Sans fonts in your books. You would not be able to gain respect, be taken seriously. Not you, as publisher, nor your authors, as writers. Now, we can certainly *choose* "older" standards and opt out of evil corporate ones, and we sure as hell might well want to: I'm inspired by a recent movement of tech folks who are choosing to create low-fi zines to reproduce their work, for example. Or quitting Facebook. You get the idea.

But for those actions to be legible as actions, they have to be *chosen;* they have to be an option. Amazon must allow people to refuse to opt-in for this gambit to work. And it does allow everyone to opt-in. Which allows, well—more competition.

So yes, Amazon has wreaked havoc on publishers, booksellers, and readers. It has had deleterious effects on book culture overall. Consumers should try to avoid purchasing books there, spending their dollars instead at independent booksellers, publishers, and other businesses to help them thrive. It should be regulated. But to say, "Amazon is pure evil and nothing it enables is worth it" is to say that small independent publishers like Belt should not exist. I think it's good that Belt was able to use the small ladder Amazon dangled to us to crawl our way up to become a larger press. Also, although I wish the percentage were much lower, about 50 percent of our sales still come from Amazon. Sadly, we require those sales to stay afloat.

For me, it seems the situation is vexing, complicated, nuanced. Amazon is a monopoly, yes—but also one that prevents other monopolies.

Preorders

Authors often confuse readers with a push/pull regarding Amazon: many beg their fans not to buy books from the megasite, only to later ask readers who enjoyed the book to write an Amazon review to help, again, with their algorithms. Poor consumers—they're just trying to make an ethical financial decision and support literary culture!

I myself have spent many hours of my life asking people to preorder books. For me, the pitch is very targeted: please preorder forthcoming titles from *our store* (beltpublishing.com— check it out!). In fact, for a while we did not list our titles on Amazon until the last minute to maximize direct sales to our online store. As we saw in the P&L in Chapter Three, we need a certain percentage of consumers to purchase books directly from us to stay in business. Also, once a book has been released, people are far more likely to go to Amazon or a bookstore to get their copy, so the best time for us to gather those direct sales is before the book officially releases.

This means that we deliberately steer people *away* from preordering via Amazon, in some sense making things harder for ourselves. Our sales numbers according to

Bookscan, the publishing industry's largest sales reporting service, will always be misleadingly low because they do not capture the 25 percent of sales we make directly to readers. In general, people in the industry will always assume we sell fewer copies than we do, which might hurt us in future advance orders that are lower than we might hope, or attention from critics and others who might look at previous sales to gauge interest in an upcoming title.

This is a loss I am fine with taking because it allows us to earn more money for each book. We are then able to publish more books and offer contracts to—you guessed it—people who are often overlooked by Big Five publishers, including women, BIPOC, and LGBTQ writers.

Returns

The single most idiosyncratic aspect of book publishing—and an eye-opener to many who don't work in it, including authors—is the returns system.

The parameters are simple: booksellers who order books at a discount through a wholesaler or distributor, including independent booksellers, Amazon, Costco, Barnes & Noble, museum gift shops, etc., can return those books for any reason at any time and receive a full or mostly-full refund. What this means for publishers is, as a fellow publisher put it to me, jokingly, "nothing is ever really sold."

Here is how that might look from the publisher's end: on a Monday in September, we receive orders for six of our newest titles (yay!) from three different vendors: Amazon, Small Bookstore in Ohio, and Baker & Taylor (another wholesaler). The amount ordered from us that day adds up to, say, $2,000 net, after all the fees are taken out (yay!). Since the distributor takes up to one hundred days to pay us for these orders, the publisher can anticipate receiving that $2,000 in January. We then make plans accordingly, perhaps offering a larger advance to an author we are courting, or paying off some printing bills.

But then, sometime in December, or the following March, one or all of those vendors might decide to return unsold books. They will receive a credit, and that credit will be taken out of the amount the distributor owes us. And it is taken out immediately, as opposed to the one hundred days later that checks are issued. We may not receive that $2,000 in January if the books are returned, which means it is dangerous to assume any cash flow that month. It is also difficult to assume cash flow for October, November, and December because copies ordered in September might be returned in those months, too, and then deducted from our account immediately.

From a financial perspective, the returns systems makes it exceedingly difficult for a publisher to subsist on cash flow because we never know *until the moment a check is deposited into our account* how much we will be receiving from our distributor in any given month. It also creates a rather bipolar cycle of excitement/disappointment as we receive large, unexpected orders only to later have, perhaps from an entirely different source, a large, unexpected number of returns.

Why do publishers acquiesce to this system? Usually they respond that the risk is worth it to have some presence on shelves to promote a title. That is, they'd rather a bookstore have a few copies they try to sell, even if unsuccessfully, than never have those copies at all. The other answer, which might be more accurate, is that the returns system is so ingrained in the bookselling industry, it would create huge conflicts to alter.

The advantage of the returns system for booksellers is obvious. For example, Main Street Bookstore decides it could sell ten copies of *Main Street Stories*. The book publishes in June, so they place an order for ten books in January because they do their ordering months in advance.

Come June, those ten copies show up. Two months pass, and they still have seven copies in stock. By October, they have five copies remaining. Their shelves are full, and *Blockbuster Book about Trump* is publishing next week, and several more customers than they anticipated have asked about copies. They decide they need more room for *Blockbuster*, so they send the five remaining copies of *Main Street Stories* back to the distributor and receive a refund.

It's a series of smart business decisions for the bookseller. Main Street Bookstore did not want to be caught empty-handed when *Main Street Stories* dropped, so they ordered plenty. There was little risk of over-ordering since they could return without penalty and would have no time pressure to decide. There is often not a clear expiration date on returns: booksellers could send them back in a week, or a year, or even longer.

But for publishers—and for eager authors checking their sales—it's a mess.

Let's back up and rewind. It is January, and a publisher is considering printer quotes for *Main Street Stories* to be published three months later. How many copies should they order? It is a guessing game. But they may receive notice of advance orders. Look, the publisher says, Main Street Bookstore placed an order for ten copies. Books Are Great Bookstore ordered four. Hipster Urban Bookstore ordered twenty. Amazon ordered two hundred. Adding up those advance orders is the best way a publisher can decide how many copies of a book to print.

At this point, bookstores and publishers are at cross-purposes to a certain extent: it costs nothing for the bookstore to over-order, but it costs the publisher plenty if it prints too many copies.

So no publisher or author should ever consider any copy of a book really "sold" until a year or so after an order is placed. Authors should be wary of initial print run estimates based on advance orders or using Amazon's Author Central book sales figures to count sales and anticipate royalties. An order is not a sale.

The returns system is less beneficial to booksellers than my above publisher-centric perspective would have it. Let's go back to that example above and look at it from the bookstore's side of things.

Let's say I owned Main Street Books and we ordered ten copies of Belt's much anticipated *Main Street Stories* in January 2018. Let's say the book's publication date is June 5 (the first Tuesday in June; books always come out on Tuesdays for some reason). Let's also say that we don't order enough from Belt to have a direct account with them and so instead we order from Big Book Distributor.

New releases typically arrive the Thursday before publicaiton date, so our ten copies of *Main Street Stories* ship on May 30 and show up on May 31 (super fast!). *Main Street Stories* is a $16 paperback and we get a 40 percent discount, meaning they cost us $9.60 each, or $96 for ten copies. Our payment terms are standard, thirty days EOM (end of month), meaning we have to pay Big Book Distributor at the end of the next month following the invoice date. In this case, June 30.

For a small press book, *Main Street Stories* does pretty well, selling five copies by October. At $16 a copy, that means we've taken in $80. But wait, we paid Big Book Distributor $96, so after five months, we have $16 less in the bank than when we started (negative cash flow).

In other words, a strategy to order ten copies of a book and return five is no way to run a bookstore. Any bookstore that routinely operated that way would be in dire financial straights very soon.

It's exhausting, returns. Not just the fact that a sale is never really a sale, or the long delay between "sale" and payment, but also the uncertainty of what will actually arrive in our bank account. (The only advice I ever give to people thinking about starting a press is one I didn't receive when I started mine: *have a lot of capital.*) Environmentalism is a hidden victim of this system as well. There is a lot of shipping back and forth baked into the system.

For my part, I've stopped raging against the return machine, as I did earlier in my still-nascent publishing career. I suppose it is a good illustration of how hegemony works, or maybe I am just that frog in a pot of boiling water. I have shifted from screaming, "Hey guys look this is absurd! We must organize to end this unfair system!" to "[shruggy guy emoji]."

Direct Sales

While I've spent a lot of time and energy trying to navigate the system of middlemen these past few years, the fact remains that the single main revenue source for Belt Publishing is direct sales through our own online store (beltpublishing. com—again, please check it out!). Without people who have decided to purchase our books from us, eliminating all the middlemen, we would not have survived. And it is those sales that have allowed us to punch above our weight ever since.

The math is pretty easy: say Jill buys a book from the Belt Publishing store. The book retails for $20, and she pays $20 to us. Yay! $20 comes into our checking account.

Now say Jill buys that same book from anywhere else: an independent bookseller, Amazon, Barnes & Noble, etc. The order goes through our distributor. The retailer—Amazon, Main Street Books, Someone Else—pays the distributor a steeply discounted price, usually between 40 and 60 percent of the retail price. For the sake of ease, let's say it is $10. So now $10 goes into our account at our distributors for the sale. The distributor takes out its fees for their services. Now we might be at $7.50 for that $20 book. And we get that money, as discussed above, 90 to 120 days later. Because of the returns system, though, that money could always be deducted from some future distributor statement.

It was very clear to me early on that we could never make the math work unless we received a healthy stream of $20 direct orders as well as the slower stream of seven bucks fifty. We have always invested a lot of energy and time directing people to our store, and we will continue to do so.

Where will it be shelved?
METADATA

Two different friends of mine were recently told by their agents that they would not send their book proposals to editors because "it wasn't clear where the book would be shelved." That is, the proposals didn't fit squarely into a preestablished category—a memoir, a history, a work of true crime, or a biography—and were instead a mix of genres. Both friends took their agents' advice and ditched their proposals, starting new ones that were more clearly geared toward one sort of genre of another.

This is a terribly impoverished approach to making a good book. In fact, it seems downright backward. Don't we want books that are original, not familiar? Aren't many of the best books those that refuse easy generic categorization, such as Claudia Rankine's *Citizen* and Maggie Nelson's *The Argonauts*, to name a few recent American examples? Isn't this set-up patronizing? Booksellers aren't dummies; they can read back cover copy and decide themselves where books should go on the shelf. And because the majority of books are sold online, doesn't that mean there are an infinite number of ways to catalog and shelve them?

I do not want a future where all books are only a variation on a preestablished theme, where every book fits in neatly to the "X meets Y" paradigm ("It's Malcolm Gladwell meets Mary Roach!" "It's Mark Kurlansky meets Bob Woodward!"). We need invention more critically than we need to recycle old models.

That said, it is true that categorizing books is often flummoxing. Every title must be accompanied by a BISAC code. BISAC stands for "Book Industry Standards and Communications," and it is the "list of standard subjects designed for use in the book trade in the U.S. and English-Speaking Canada." There are 3,000 of them, and they are updated periodically. In short, BISAC tells people, and algorithms, where to shelve books.

BISAC includes major categories, such as Architecture, Medical, Poetry, Foreign Language Study, and each of these contains dozens of subcategories. If you choose Architecture as your BISAC, for example, you then have to choose one of forty-one additional options, including Architecture/Building/Residential; Architecture/Decoration & Ornament; Architecture/History/Medieval, Architecture/Individual Architects & Firms, Monographs, Architecture/Urban & Land Use Planning; Architecture/History/Modern (late 19th Century to 1945).

Confusingly, BISAC codes are not the same as Library of Congress designations, a system that I, as a former academic, took a long time to get my head around. Nor are they the same as Amazon's purely market-driven algorithmic categories, which can make many writers feel they have written a bestseller when that little orange banner appears by the title ("#1 in Midwest Travel Guides!" or "#29 in Human Geography!").

Publishing is a trendy business, perhaps too much so, and categories rise and fall—in one year, outdated the next, and back in style another five years from now. Some of those trends, if they gain enough popularity, eventually become new BISACs.

CHAPTER SEVEN:

Selling Books

A writer with a huge Twitter following had a book coming out soon and she tweeted this question: "I need to start planning book marketing stuff so tell me, what is one thing you wished you knew about selling a book that I should know?"

My response: "Public radio sells books."

I have written three books. I've published forty of them. Based on this wildly unscientific sample, I don't hesitate to declare that for certain kinds of books, public radio is the main driver of book sales. How do I know? I get to see the back end. I can see Amazon rankings for titles go from 1,243,302 to 7,900; I can see bookstore orders coming in on the distributor dashboard; I can, if it is a Belt book, see those delicious direct store orders flow in, causing Bill Rickman, who does our shipping, to groan, and me to smile at his annoyance.

There are caveats to my argument, of course: I write and publish the sorts of books public radio listeners like. I have no idea what methods and outlets are best for marketing celebrity biographies, or romance novels, or business books, or Mandarin dictionaries. I'm referring mainly to serious and narrative nonfiction, history, literary fiction, and the other genres you might see covered in the *New York Times Book Review* or other similar outlets.

Of that most prominent of book review outlets, the *New York Times Book Review*, I'd place it in the second tier on my list of things that contribute to sales. It gives books a prestige, and using pull quotes from a *New York Times* review on a book's back cover can certainly drive sales. But for immediate gratification—a book's rank increasing on Amazon, the generation of more bookstore orders—it's been surprisingly lackluster in my experience.

There are other common forms of book marketing that are also less useful than they might seem: creating a flashy author website; creating a Facebook page for your book; writing "book adjacent" essays and op-eds that go live around the book's publication date (especially if those essays are unpaid, as they often are); bookstore appearances (though these do generate goodwill, can be super-fun, and may help your book be hand-sold to others later).

So then, after public radio, what is the second most effective form of book marketing in my limited experience?

Word of mouth.

I am so cheered by this because it goes against the enervating drumbeat of so much other conventional wisdom out there: that authors have to be their own publicists, that authorial hustling is the key to sales, and that promoting a book has to be a full-time job for six months. Many people claim that publishers have abdicated their duties as marketers and booksellers and are instead making authors do everything. But maybe it is neither publishers nor authors—nor media—that actually creates buzz. Maybe, if a great book finds the right reader, that reader will tell another reader who will tell another, and then suddenly the book appears on a bestseller list.

Okay, maybe it doesn't happen exactly like that.

Word of mouth is a little more intangible. And often it involves Twitter. But I have seen it happen often enough that it has led me to disregard a lot of conventional wisdom and industry practices.

For word of mouth to spur sales, the book has to be really good. That might seem like an obvious statement, but there are a lot of overhyped, mediocre books out there. They get a lot of initial buzz and a lot of initial sales. But a book with a strong voice, an interesting story, and a tight manuscript put together by a confident author and confident editors can cause serious readers to take notice. Those people, be they your voracious reading neighbor, an editor at a literary publication, or someone with a six digit Twitter following, will tell people about the book. Then those people will read it, suggest it to their followers and book clubs, and create momentum.

But the author or someone else—an "influencer" or a critic or just a loudmouthed friend with reach—needs to get that initial word out. And that initial step can be random and unpredictable.

When the author I mentioned at the beginning of this chapter tweeted her question to her thousands of followers, people replied. She responded to their replies, thanking them, making jokes. Other ears perked up. More people on Twitter, like me, saw the thread, and, curious, checked her Twitter bio for the title of the book she was about to start marketing. We looked it up on Amazon or Googled it. Maybe some of us preordered it. Maybe there were some of us who also work in media, and we sent an email to the book's editor, seeing if we could cover the book when it published.

The tweet itself helped market the book. An interesting person with 25,000 followers was sincerely asking for help, and then taking the time to respond to strangers' suggestions. I wager she sold fifty or so copies, indirectly or directly, with one tweet that didn't even mention the title of her book.

Now you might say, "But she has so many followers! I only have 135." But one main reason this author has so many followers is because she is engaging. Word about her book got out because she accomplished something intangible. It's not something you can study, and it's not something you can ever try to emulate. It's only the first step, of course: once the book comes out, readers get to weigh in, and if the book is good, they will do more work on the book's behalf. But if it is not, word of mouth will still happen, but this time it'll take the form of a general hush, a drop in the rankings, and an uptick in bookstore returns.

Your Platform

"Ugh, I really should get on Twitter."

I often hear this from people who have a book coming out. They have dutifully thought about how authors should help promote books, and Twitter often lands at the top of the list for go-to strategies. This is for good reason—a good Twitter presence can definitely move copies. But it's not nearly as simple as tweeting "BUY MY BOOK!" again and again.

It's much more nuanced than that. And it isn't going to happen if you're reluctantly approaching Twitter as something you *should* do. Do not—I repeat, DO NOT—create or revive a Twitter account solely in order to help with book promotion. It would be like showing up at a cocktail party where you don't know anyone and then going up to each guest and saying, "Hey, here is my book. Please buy it." People will come to know who you are, but they probably won't like you all that much.

However, if you know the people at the cocktail party and you've been engrossed in other conversations with them for a long time, and *then* you mention that you have a book publishing in a month, chances are your friends will think, "OMG, I need to buy this! I also need to tell all my friends about it!"

This is why a good Twitter presence—one done for nonselfish reasons—can be a great thing for authors.

But authors can do many other things to help sell books besides tweet about them. And, yes, if authors devote the right time and energy, they can sell more copies of their books than if they did nothing, or if they did the wrong things. That's because authors offer what no one else—not the editor, publicist, distributor, or book reviewer—can.

So what, other than Twitter, can an author do to create a "platform"—that insidious catch-all term for a variety of things, such as having a prestigious job, being a media figure or influencer, heading a large organization, or being a pundit? But for our purposes, think about a platform like this: What can an author do, before the book publishes, to help sell copies?

Here are some examples from my recent experience:

1) An editor of one of Belt's city anthologies knew the local media, and he worked it. He sent lots of emails and follow-ups to help us, and our publicist, get local coverage for the book. His efforts worked, the book sold well, and we were all deeply appreciative.

2) A friend of mine had a book coming out soon and hated social media. He asked me for advice. The book was about a community based around a medical condition, so I asked him if that community knew about him and the book. He said yes. I suggested he work those networks, instead of media/social media, and reach out to email listservs and online forums where this group hung out, letting them know about the book and asking them to help spread the word.

3) Are you friendly with your local bookstore? Do you buy a lot of books there? (The answer should be yes.) Talk with them. One bookstore can hand-sell a lot of copies. It is likely the bookseller has bookseller friends, and if your book is good, it will warrant a mention. Booksellers like to "discover" talent or help promote worthy books that might otherwise be overlooked.

4) Do you have friends? Email them, post about the book on Facebook, or go wherever they hang out. Ask them if they would preorder the book, explaining why that's important, and offer them something if they do. One friend of mine sent a signed galley page to everyone who preordered his book (including me). It feels good to do nice things for friends.

5) Send copies of your book, or any publicity info, as soon as it arrives, with little notes, to people you think would be interested, and who might mention it to their influential friends. Hand-sell your book by thinking about why a person might be interested—other than being nice to you.

I have complicated thoughts about publishing "book-adjacent" essays and the like, which are things many publishers pressure authors to do, because it often means unpaid labor for the author, and it has mixed results. But every time I'm about to say "never doing that again," someone publishes an excerpt or book-related essay that clearly sells a bunch of copies for Belt, making me think twice.

But to back up a bit: the rise of the pressure to have a "platform" parallels the rise in major publishers seeking to publish books by celebrities. I'm not in that game at all, so I have a different calculus when I think about whether or not an author might help sell copies of a book I am considering signing.

First, do I think a book will find its audience, and then be so damn good that the audience will do the marketing work for us? To decide this, I first ascertain the book's quality (duh), and then I think about whether or not Belt can help the book find its readers. For instance, is it a book about urbanism, the Rust Belt, a certain kind of intellectual history, or a lefty political topic? If so, we can probably get it to readers interested in those topics, and then see how those readers respond, crossing our fingers that they'll agree with our assessment that the book is amazing. But if the book is about, say, religious mysticism or Islamic history, I worry that no matter how good it is, we won't be able to help it find its people.

Ultimately, it's about horizontal loyalty. Fuck platforms. I mean, really. Fuck them. The term connotes a vertical, top-down relationship between author and reader. The readers below will look up to the author on high and buy their book. That might work for some authors and some publishing houses, but I am a proponent of working very, very hard on horizontal loyalty, the idea that you should focus your attention and support on those on a similar plane to you career-wise, networking with them instead of seeking to impress those "above" you. Similarly, author and reader could meet on the same level. I like to work with authors who feel the same. Let's all be on the same ground together. When we do that, we'll all rise together too.

Maybe that's hokey. But I'm not running Belt as some "labor of love" or a "passion project." When people say that about Belt, I bristle. I love and am passionate about what we do, but we are also committed to selling lots of copies and making money too. We are not doing favors here; I'm a small business owner. I just happen to also believe that horizontal loyalty isn't just a good way to develop relationships and exist in the world, it's also a good way to make money.

Marketing and Publicity

At Belt we develop publicity and marketing plans for all our titles. As I was writing this chapter, I also spent a big part of the week doing that for our spring 2020 titles. We planned to send press releases, galleys, and catalogs to media and bookstores.

We signed up for booths at book fairs and trade shows. We scheduled readings. We even thought about taking out some ads. We tried to be clever about touting our titles on social media. And of course we did everything we could to get public radio—local, state, or national—to cover the titles.

The connection between media coverage and book sales is much more tenuous than you would expect. Sometimes, copious national media can lead to few sales. In other cases, a book will sell like crazy despite receiving no press.

I've been on both sides of this equation. The first book I published (that is, the first book I wrote and someone else published) was *A Skeptic's Guide to Writers' Houses,* which came out in 2010. The University of Pennsylvania Press published it as a trade title (that is, a title that was meant for the "general public," and not a peer-reviewed book primarily geared toward academics), and I was gobsmacked with the media reception. The *Wall Street Journal* reviewed it (and liked it!); so did the *Chicago Tribune.* It was reviewed in the *New York Review of Books* (they didn't like it so much). I even pitched and placed a book-adjacent essay in the *New York Times Book Review* that published the same month my book came out! It was all a thrill.

It sold very few copies.

In 2012, I published my first book (that is, a book that others wrote and I published) called *The Cleveland Anthology.* It was self-published—or, well, teensy-tiny-small-press published. It received no national coverage, no reviews, just a few mentions in local publications. Within two months it sold more copies than *A Skeptic's Guide* had in the previous two years. Within three months, it sold through its first printing of two thousand copies. It is currently in its second edition and its fifth printing.

A Skeptic's Guide was a complete and total success for me: it was life-changing. I proved something to myself by writing it. I proved something to my professional colleagues at the college where I taught. It launched what would become an entirely new career for me. That an astonishingly small number of people actually bought the book did not matter to me. It did, however, matter to my publisher, who likely had anticipated greater sales.

What's the lesson here? For me, this experience got me wondering if I was better—at least in terms of sheer numbers—at being a publisher than an author. For everyone else: never assume a correlation between press coverage and sales numbers. For instance, this morning I read an article in the *New York Times* business section about late-night hosts inviting authors on to their shows and the boost that provides. The story contained sales figures for some of the best-selling, Trump-related titles of the year. Then I logged into the Bookscan database—password-protected and accessible only through a subscription—that gives sales figures for every book sold, and I searched the sales numbers for the less famous folks mentioned in the article. For the most part, all the sales reported there were lower than the capacity of Madison Square Garden. It was far fewer than you might expect is what I'm saying.

However, as I mentioned in Chapter Six, these numbers are unreliable. It is insanely confusing to count book sales because many sales are not reported, and many orders for books are later returned, so book sales histories look more like a stock market graph. And there are so many factors to weigh when you're trying to decide if a certain number of sales is "good" or "bad" (What genre? Which press? How much was the advance?). But here's my take: if you are a literary novelist and you sell 1,000 to 2,000 copies, you are doing okay, despite what you might feel. If you sell 3,000 to 5,000, your publisher is probably not upset. If you sell 10,000, you are probably beating most of your Twitter friends, even if they seem to keep getting more press or awards than you are. You'll also probably have an easier time getting a second book contract with a Big Five publisher.

For nonfiction, the numbers trend a tad, but not much, higher. In 2016, I wrote (and another publisher published) my second book, *The History and Uncertain History of Handwriting*. It was also a work of nonfiction, published by a larger press than my first, with a much, much, much larger advance. I also placed a book adjacent op-ed with the *New York Times* and the book received coverage in the *New York Times Book Review*. I have never received a four-figure royalty check for this book.

But as a publisher at Belt, I write such royalty checks to many of our authors who have not received national press. The system can work.

What I ask prospective authors to consider before signing with us is this: What is your goal for a book? Is it to just write a book and have it printed on paper? Are you writing it in order to get tenure or a promotion? Is it to take part in an ongoing conversation? Is it to get a large advance so you can take a leave from work?

If your goal is to make money, the most surefire way to do that is to land the largest advance you can (the odds are still very small, though, and largely out of your control). Likewise, there are many indirect ways to make money from a book in addition to different or better jobs: invited talks, commissioned articles, second book contracts, consultancies, selling reprint rights. I have earned a nice, steady stream of such revenue from the books I have written.

A publisher, of course, has to make a different calculus: will we recoup our costs with a book's sales? The number of copies we sell doesn't answer that question. The answer really lies in how much we spend on the book. Selling one hundred copies of a particular title can lead to more profit than selling 10,000 copies of another. It's nothing fancy: it's simply the relationship between the amount you spend on a book divided by the number of copies sold. Spend less, and you can profit from selling just a few hundred copies. But if you spend too much, you might need to sell 20,000 copies simply to break even.

Galleys

Galleys are copies of titles that are printed before publication for the media and other readers the publisher wants to give an early look. In the industry, a galley goes by a number of names: an ARC (Advance Reading Copy), a reader copy, or a proof. They are marked as such, usually with a sticker or a notice on the front that reads: ADVANCE UNCORRECTED COPY. They are never sold (and have no barcode), and they might be missing a few elements, such as an acknowledgments section or endnotes. They also usually contain typos and errors that will be corrected in the proofreading process before the final copies are printed. Publishers produce galleys from two months to one year before the book's official publication date. They're sent to media, prospective blurbers, and influential people, given away at bookseller trade shows, sent to distributor sales representatives and bookstore buyers, and offered as giveaways to Goodreads or Amazon readers.

Galleys are important for securing prepublication or trade reviews at *Publishers Weekly*, *Kirkus*, *Library Journal*, and other outlets that write thumbnail reviews of forthcoming titles. Librarians, booksellers, and reviewers read these publications to help them choose from the tens of thousands of books published each month in the United States.

Not all publishers make galleys, and they'll often order different quantities of galleys for different titles. Publishers make this decision based on a title's sales projection. Conglomerate publishers might print more galleys for a title than a smaller press will print for an entire print run. Likewise, that same conglomerate might print thousands of galleys for the newest book by a big name author, but only a few dozen galleys for a book of short stories by a lesser-known name. Small presses and university presses often do not print any galleys at all.

More modest sales projections aren't the only reason a press might decide to forego galleys. University presses, for example, can be reasonably certain they can find an audience for their books without them. Some titles, such as how-to guides, are unlikely to benefit from advance promotion simply because it's unlikely those kinds of books will garner media attention. For small presses, one of the driving reasons they choose to print only a small number of galleys—or to print none at all—is cost.

As I discussed earlier, printing operates on a steep economy of scale; the more you print, the cheaper it costs per copy. Galleys, since they are printed in smaller batches, are thus always proportionally more expensive. The costs involved in shipping galleys can be sizeable as well. If Belt ships 300 galleys for a title, for example, we will spend about $1,000 in postage, plus another $500 to $1,000 or so in materials, handling fees, and labor. When we create the P&L for a title, if we have decided to make galleys, we need to add at least $2,500 to our marketing budget, which means we need to sell hundreds of additional copies of the final book to break even.

Galleys are marketing material, and marketing is always a risk. Sometimes, galleys turn out to be money well-spent—positive reviews, larger orders, or reviews in places like *Kirkus* that give the title more attention. Sometimes, though, they turn out to be money wasted. For some of our titles, Belt has sent out hundreds of galleys and received no media coverage. Conversely, we have outstripped all our sales projections for titles that did not have galleys.

Regular book reviewers will sometimes post photos on Twitter of gigantic stacks of advance copies publishers have sent to them. Editors will sometimes showcase the piles and piles and piles of galleys they receive every day. As an independent publisher, these photos are painful to see because it means the odds our book will be chosen for review are miniscule. So why even send a reviewer one more slim title—one that has maybe a 5 percent chance of being looked at, not to mention read—to be added to this pile? Especially when it costs us so much, in money and labor and increased pressure on our schedule, to produce?

Galleys are yet another example of publishing's uneven playing field: independent presses have a harder time than conglomerates getting advance buzz for their titles because it costs us proportionately more money to do so.

What makes this system even more frustrating is that, unlike the returns system, the entire current galley calculus, and the unequal distribution of eyeballs on advance copies, could pretty easily be wiped out without injuring anyone involved in this economy. Currently, there is an alternate way to get as many advance copies of a book to everybody who could possibly benefit a press. And it doesn't cost a thing. No printing costs. No shipping costs. No additional expenses in the marketing budget. It's called e-galleys.

Belt can send a digital file of any book to a limitless number of people in the media. They are easily attached to emails, which can then be transferred to e-reading devices for free. Plus, e-galleys are much healthier for the environment.

Unfortunately, eight times out of ten, the person interested in a title specifically requests a print copy. Some prepublication outlets require printed copies. In response to our offers of PDFs, many media contacts respond with, "I don't like to read on a screen," or, "We have a policy of print galleys only."

Authors are sometimes disappointed if I decide not to make galleys of their titles. They see them, often rightly so, as a sign of our taking the title seriously. Reviewers and buyers, plus our distributor sales reps, aren't happy when we don't make galleys, either. But if more publishers would offer only e-galleys, the tide would turn, and whoosh!— the whole galley economy would crash. Wouldn't that be a better, more valuable way—financially, environmentally, and otherwise—to spend the balance in our checking account? And wouldn't it be an easy way to help redress the inequality of attention that currently exists between conglomerate and independent presses?

Author Events

Some months, my calendar is dominated by traveling to author events. In one ten-day stretch in June 2019, I traveled to DC, Milwaukee, and St. Louis to celebrate Belt book releases. It was my most anticipated week of the year because launch parties are my favorite part of my job, mostly because they involve, well, parties. But it's also because of the particular celebratory joy of a crowd gathered to celebrate a writer or writers, the support they show for their friend or family member, and the writers' pride that they try to hide but end up revealing anyway, particularly in their furtive smiles when they think no one else is looking.

It is difficult to time when you should celebrate the completion of a book. There are either no markers—or too many of them—of "done." There is the "done" when you finish your manuscript and send it to your editor. But then you receive edits and have to start writing again. After that, you still have to review page proofs. Then, once the text is finalized, you have to shift into promotion mode—the writing may be done but the "book" has not even started yet. The first advance copies of the book arrive. "Look! It's real!" you might brag on social media. But a galley still isn't the final version.

To me, the best way to really mark and celebrate the completion and achievement of book writing is with a launch party, especially if it is one filled with exceedingly prideful mothers, husbands, children, and the like. The high I receive from attending always helps get me through the next crisis or bureaucratic annoyance, be it a cash flow crunch or a distribution screwup.

However, when it comes to book events per se—after or beyond any official launch party—I don't believe that quantity should always be the goal, or that an author has to say yes to any offer that comes her way to maximize publicity and sales. And I do not encourage devoting an inordinate amount of time to setting up readings at bookstores or devoting resources to travel from one to the next.

I may catch some flak for this position. For example, booksellers won't be happy because they benefit from hosting author events. And I may well be wrong in my approach. But explaining it might alleviate some worries and pressures that writers and other independent publishers might have.

I do not encourage writers to plan lengthy tours or set up dozens of smaller, discrete events over the course of a few months primarily because most writers have other work they have to do while they are promoting their books. Many of them also have family obligations. And the potential bottom-line upside of an event (media coverage and book sales) is usually not high enough to warrant the disruption the event would cause.

When my first book was published, I was a college professor in the middle of a very busy semester, as well as a single parent for a school-age child. To promote my book at the half dozen or so events that my publisher helped line up for me, I had to cancel and reschedule many classes, find someone to take care of my son while I was away, find time to fulfill the other obligations of my day job (grading, preparing classes, attending department meetings), and pay for many of the flights and hotels myself. It was difficult to arrange, and it was stressful overall.

Don't get me wrong, I had fun at these events, and I was so grateful for my hosts and everyone who attended. (They had actually left the house just to sit in a chair and listen to me talk!) It was all a bit unimaginable and glamorous and dream-fulfilling. But having to manage so much was also overwhelming and exhausting. If doing it would have increased my chances to sell a lot of books—and to receive additional royalties in a year or so—it would have been a good trade-off. But the number of copies I sold at these events, and the number most people sell at most of their readings, is relatively small, especially compared to the number of copies one might sell with a strong review, or an essay about the book an author might place in a publication read by millions, or one person with five million Twitter followers posting a rave review, or friends mentioning to their other friends that they read an amazing book that everyone should read. Like retail politics, selling books in real life, copy by copy, is good for community, good for the soul, and good for the long arc of a career. But in reality, it rarely leads to enough direct sales in the short time of a promotion window to make up for the immense amount of energy, labor, and resources an author and/or her publicist must invest.

Having now promoted three books that I have written, I have discovered, somewhat to my surprise, that, in addition to the issues outlined above, readings drain me more than they energize. Other writers, however, have the opposite reaction. In fact, for some people, the prospect of book events and being "on tour" can be a prime motivator for finishing the damn book (we all need something to keep us going!). For these authors, the event cycle of book publishing is the most anticipated, coveted, and enjoyable aspect of the job. The number of copies they sell may be ancillary, and maybe having other people cover family obligations provides a needed respite. They may not have a day job, or they may have one that is flexible yet isolating, so the prospect of meeting new people on the road is a boon. Maybe their publisher is underwriting all the costs, or maybe they have plenty of money to pay for travel without hardship.

The conventional wisdom in publishing—or at least the commonly assumed presumption—is that more is better. So many authors assume they should be out there hustling at events to make their publishers happy. Many will do outreach and say yes to invitations because they want to show their publishers they are good soldiers, willing to do their part to sell the book.

But my wisdom, such as it is, is less conventional. I believe the number of book events an author should attend must be intimately connected to the author's particular situation and preferences. If someone hates to travel, she should not feel pressure to visit eight states in eight days. If someone has small children and/or a demanding day job, maybe they shouldn't do any bookstore readings. Nor should people who have social anxiety be forced to counter their own inclinations unless it is clearly merited (such as an invited lecture or an awards presentation).

There are other things authors can do from their couches, and whenever they can grab the time that would be just as beneficial for sales. Social media, reaching out to contacts and networking through email, and writing pieces for publication around the time of the book's release are all convenient and fairly easy to do. And they're oftentimes more profitable than more conventional author events.

There is a third approach to author events and readings that is the ideal scenario: have the host underwrite travel, pay an honorarium, and schedule the event when it is convenient for the author. Universities and libraries often invite speakers and offer honoraria and/or travel stipends. Unlike bookstores, which tend to schedule readings months before a book is published to time them with the book's release, universities often invite authors after a book's publication, when there is interest among faculty, students, or administrators who have read the book, and when the author is under less stress to promote the title.

A strategy where an author does a few readings around the book's publication date to celebrate the moment of the book's arrival—the launch party!—and then solicits invitations to join built-in communities (college courses, society meetings) to do readings for a fee in the year after the book's publication, and to discuss the book itself—not just hawk a product—can be an indirect way a publisher, especially an independent one, can help authors make more money from their book-writing labor.

Making Money from Books

How much can you actually make from writing a book? It is true that a book can make you a millionaire. And you can do that in two ways. First, you could get a multimillion dollar advance against royalties. You can also sell enough copies of your book to receive a million dollars in royalties. This also happens!

You will not, however, necessarily become a millionaire by getting a book on the bestseller list. To hit the list, you only have to sell about 10,000 copies of a book in one week (and actually, there is no one answer to how to hit the *New York Times* bestseller list, which doesn't actually count the books that sold the most, and 10,000 may not be the number, even if they do count yours). No matter what the "actual" answer is to how many books you have to sell in a week to make the bestseller list once, it still won't make you a millionaire. However, if you stay on the bestseller list for a year or so? Now you're talking!

Answering the question about how to make money from books is a little like asking, "How much should you expect to sell your house for?" Think of all the different variables involved. How big a house is it? Where is it? What's the market like? Does it have granite countertops?

But I will go through a few scenarios to try to answer these questions.

First up: if you sign up for *Publishers Marketplace*, you can access reports of some recent book deals. There is a specific language used in the marketplace: a "nice" deal means an advance of $1–$49,000; a "very nice deal" is $50,000–$99,000; a "good deal" is $100,000–$250,000; a "significant deal" is $251,000–$499,000; and a "major deal" is $500,000 and up. Let's imagine an author receives a $25,000 advance. Nice! If there was an agent representing the writer, she will usually get 15 percent of that. So now the author has about $21,000. That amount will likely be paid in three or four installments. A common plan for a book advance looks like this: 25 percent upon signing the contract, 50 percent upon acceptance of the manuscript, and the final 25 percent upon publication.

What many of us forget—me included, when I am wearing my author hat—is that the operative word here is "advance." In theory, the publisher has calculated how many copies they think a book will sell, and they've provided a percentage of those eventual sales to the author up front in order to entice them to sign the contract. A common royalty rate for a hardcover book is 10 percent; if a book retails for $20, the author would receive $2 for every copy sold. If a publisher thinks a book will sell 50,000 copies, the author's royalties would total $100,000.

Only a small fraction of books that receive major advances like this actually "earn out," selling enough copies to recoup the money the publisher fronted to the author. A corporate publisher can pay nine exceedingly big advances for every one that makes money. For many presses, that is, one book underwrites every nine they publish. Major publishers are always writing down losses. It's baked into their business model.

So, if you want to make enough money to spend one year writing a book, then you need to convince an agent, first, and then a major publisher, to offer you an advance large enough for what you need for that year (but remember: your advance will be paid out in installments). However, you should not expect to make any money on your book other than that advance, because most likely the publisher will overpay for your book, and you will never see royalties.

Now, let's flip the scenario. Say you sign with an independent press like Belt, or any press that offers you a smaller advance. You receive a modest $1,000. Your book gets published, and people buy it. The publisher sells 10,000 copies. If your royalty is 10 percent of a $20 list price, you will receive $2 per copy, or $19,000 (you received the first $1,000 up front).

There are many other factors to consider. Maybe you'll sell the book's foreign rights. You might sell audio rights. Or movie rights! Also, having a book under your belt might lead to a better job, or paid consulting gigs, or speaker fees. If your first book sells well, maybe your next book deal will come with a larger advance.

Some authors choose to trade the prospect of a higher advance for the advantages of working with an independent press and in the hopes they will receive money in royalties after the book has been published. They usually spend less time trying to sell the book before they receive a contract because they may not need an agent or an elaborate proposal, like they often would to garner a five- or six-figure advance. Signing with an independent press might involve a briefer proposal and a month of back-and-forth, instead of six months and numerous editorial board meetings. Smaller advances mean a publisher is investing less up front, so there are lower stakes to green-light a project. The acquisition process is usually simpler and quicker.

The way book publishing is discussed in the US today, royalties are often a forgotten side issue because so much emphasis is put on the advance.

For the Big Five publishers, huge conglomerates all, writing off an overly large advance that never earns out is simply routine. For independent presses, this reality creates some difficulties because most of them are unable to offer large advances. We simply can't cover losses so easily. We cannot publish four books we expect to lose money on just to get that fifth one that will bring in huge profits. Thus, authors eager to score large advances are wary of independent presses. But to receive a large advance, you have to put in months of work to write an extensive proposal—sixty to eighty pages is probably average—secure an agent, revise the proposal upon the agent's suggestions, then wait for the agent to send the proposal out to editors. That is uncompensated time. If more authors thought this way, that "big" advance might not seem quite so big after all.

How to Make Booksellers Swoon

Reporting Bookstore: This term was suggested by someone on Twitter when I was crowdsourcing for this glossary, and I'm happy she did. A reporting bookstore tells Bookscan how many copies of a title it has sold. Bookscan is the Nielsen ratings of publishing: it records book sales. Authors can access it through their Amazon author pages if they have one. Anyone can buy an extremely expensive license and access it.

Bookscan numbers don't tell the whole story. According to their own description, they count about 85 percent of books sold. Not all bookstores report their numbers; those that do are called reporting bookstores. Truly savvy publishers and authors can attempt to flood the cashiers of reporting bookstores with their books. But in addition to bookstores that do not report sales to Bookscan are a slew of other means through which people can buy nonreported books. A key to Belt Publishing's business model is enticing people to buy our books directly from our online store. We sell anywhere from from 10 to 50 percent of all copies of a book sold through our store.

ARCs and Galleys: There are long and short definitions of these terms. The long one would explain the difference between them. The short one—this one—will tell you they are interchangeable. ARC stands for Advance Reading Copy, and galley is a cooler term that contains history: printers used to place type into metal trays called galleys and run off a few copies that would then be proofed by editors. Then the printer would rearrange the letters and type in the tray upon receiving edits and reset the final version.

Both terms are frequently used today, and interchangeably, to refer to prepublication versions of books. These are sent to book reviewers, media, booksellers, and anyone who warrants a peek at the book before its publication date. ARCs and galleys are often made before a final proofreading pass, and they might lack footnotes, maps, or other elements that the final copy (or the version that will go on sale) will include. They lack barcodes or prices and are not made for retail sale. They can be used as markers of prestige. Read one on the subway to show how much of an insider you are! But never publish or publicly discuss material found in a galley before the publication date, kids! Also, never, ever sell a galley—I'm talking to you, people who list them as third-party sellers on Amazon! When you do, you take away not one, but two sales from the publisher.

Conclusion

I finished the manuscript for this book on March 1, 2020. Well, I almost finished it. I was having a difficult time deciding how to conclude, so I sent it into the production process: we edited and proofed it, and we decided how to handle design elements such as glossaries and charts. I gave myself two weeks to finish the conclusion, which would be dropped into the manuscript later.

I am writing this conclusion on March 28, 2020. The landscape of publishing has altered drastically since the beginning of this month, and in yet-unknown ways. The only conclusion I can draw today is the certainty of change.

Books have so many advantages over other more fluid forms of media, but their very distinction—that they endure, that the text inside is set—is a hurdle to my ability to sum up what is intended to be a useful peek inside an industry, as of March 2020, that may be unrecognizable to anyone reading this in 2030, or 2022, or even—primarily—those of you reading this in 2020.

What I do expect, or at least hope for, is that smaller, more flexible, and nimbler independent publishers will emerge as an ever more important alternative for authors, editors, designers, agents, and publishing professionals. The ability to control the means of production, after all, has long been a rallying cry; this extends to the means of reproduction as well. Publishing has for too long held on to archaic practices; let's smash them and reinvent new ways to make and sell books. Publishing was vastly different in ancient Rome than it was in nineteenth-century England, and midcentury American publishers had little in common with those who printed Dickens's triple-deckers. It could be fun, and good, to see how publishing might change yet again.

Michael Erard, an author and writer, said this of the current state of conglomerate publishing, in contrast to the work he has chosen to do:

> I think many publishers, editors, and agents hunger to be part of The Conversation, and that really limits what they want to publish from everyone else who's not part of The Conversation. They're publishing for a Twitter world.. . . As a writer, I'm writing for the library. So are others, I reckon. I'm making culture in longer terms, in a broader scope.

Here's to making culture that lasts, through a medium that has proven flexible enough to adapt to vastly different civilizations and societies for millennia, and that has obsessed me, personally, through my various ages and careers. And here's to doing so ethically, inventively, and independently.

A Note about the Text

The main text of the book is set in the font Adobe Garamond at 11pt size, with 13pt line spacing. Headings and drop caps are set in Butler Bold.

We have also strategically placed 7 typographical errors throughout the book for the aspiring proofreaders among you. If you think you've found them all, check out the answer key at beltpublishing.com/SYWTPABtypos.

Acknowledgments

I would not have been able to write this book without the people who created and steered Belt Publishing with me: Jim Babcock, Martha Bayne, Michelle Blankenship, Dan Crissman, Michael Jauchen, Meredith Pangrace, Bill Rickman, and David Wilson. We owe so much to the editors and authors who have published books with us, fellow-travelers in this crazy, wonderful experiment. The readers of my newsletter, Notes from a Small Press, led me turn those weekly missives into a book; thanks to all of you. To the cohort of readers and supporters who understood what Belt was trying to do back in 2013, continue to support us, and let us know we matter: it is for you we do what we do, happily. Together we have created community and meaningful work, the greatest gifts. I am indebted, grateful, and humbled.

About the Author

Anne Trubek is the founder and publisher of Belt Publishing, as well as the author of *The History and Uncertain Future of Handwriting* and *A Skeptic's Guide To Writers' Houses*, editor of *Voices From the Rust Belt*, *The Cleveland Neighborhood Guidebook*, and *Rust Belt Chic: The Cleveland Anthology*. She also founded and served as editor-in-chief of *Belt Magazine*, served on the board of the National Book Critics Circle, and was Associate Professor of Rhetoric & Composition at Oberlin College. She lives in Cleveland.

These blank pages are here to complete the signature, bringing the total page count to 160 (a number divisible by 16).